creative elem

Valerie Evans

Acknowledgements

The author and publishers would like to thank Tanya Gell and the staff at Grove Park Primary School, and Anita Ransley and the staff at Strand-on-the-Green Infant School for their help and support during the making of this book. They would also like to thank the children of these schools for their wonderful contributions of art and language work, in particular Suzannah and Grace Evans who contributed more than most!

'What am I?' (page 19)

First published in 2001 by BELAIR PUBLICATIONS LIMITED
Apex Business Centre, Boscombe Road, Dunstable, Beds, LU5 4RL

© 2001 Folens on behalf of the author Valerie Evans

Commissioning Editor: Karen McCaffery   Editor: Elizabeth Miles
Design: Jane Conway   Photography: Kelvin Freeman   Cover design: Martin Cross
Illustrators: Jane Conway pp 3, 14; Jean de Lemos pp 5, 21, 37, 53; Linda Rogers Associates: Sara Silcock p 71.

Belair books are protected by international copyright laws. All rights are reserved. The copyright of all materials in this book, except where otherwise stated, remains the property of the publisher and author. No part of this publication may be reproduced, stored in a retrieval system, or transmitted, in any form or by any means, for whatever purpose, without the written permission of Belair Publications Limited.

Every effort has been made to contact copyright holders of material used in this book. If any have been overlooked, we will be pleased to make the necessary arrangements.

Dragonbirth © Judith Nicholls 1994 from STORM's EYE by Judith Nicholls, published by Oxford University Press. Reprinted by permission of the author.

Five Haiku © Gina Douthwaite from Let's Celebrate, published by Oxford University Press. Reprinted by permission of the author.

Put on your Thinking Hat! © Judith Nicholls 1990 from HIGGELDY-HUMBUG by Judith Nicholls, published by Mary Glasgow Publications. Reprinted by permission of the author.

Picture Credits
p12: *The Burning of the Houses of Parliament*, 16th October 1834, c.1835 (oil on canvas) by Joseph Mallord William Turner (1775–1851), Philadelphia Museum of Art, Pennsylvania, PA, USA/Bridgeman Art Library; p28: *The Wave*, c.1871 by Gustav Courbet (1819-77), National Gallery of Scotland, Edinburgh, Scotland/Bridgeman Art Library; p44: *Wheatfield with Cypresses*, 1889 (oil on canvas) by Vincent van Gogh (1853–90), National Gallery, London, UK/Bridgeman Art Library; p60: *View of Toledo* by El Greco (Domenico Theotocopuli) (1541–1614), Metropolitan Museum of Art, New York, USA/Index/Bridgeman Art Library.

ISBN 0 94788 286 3

Contents

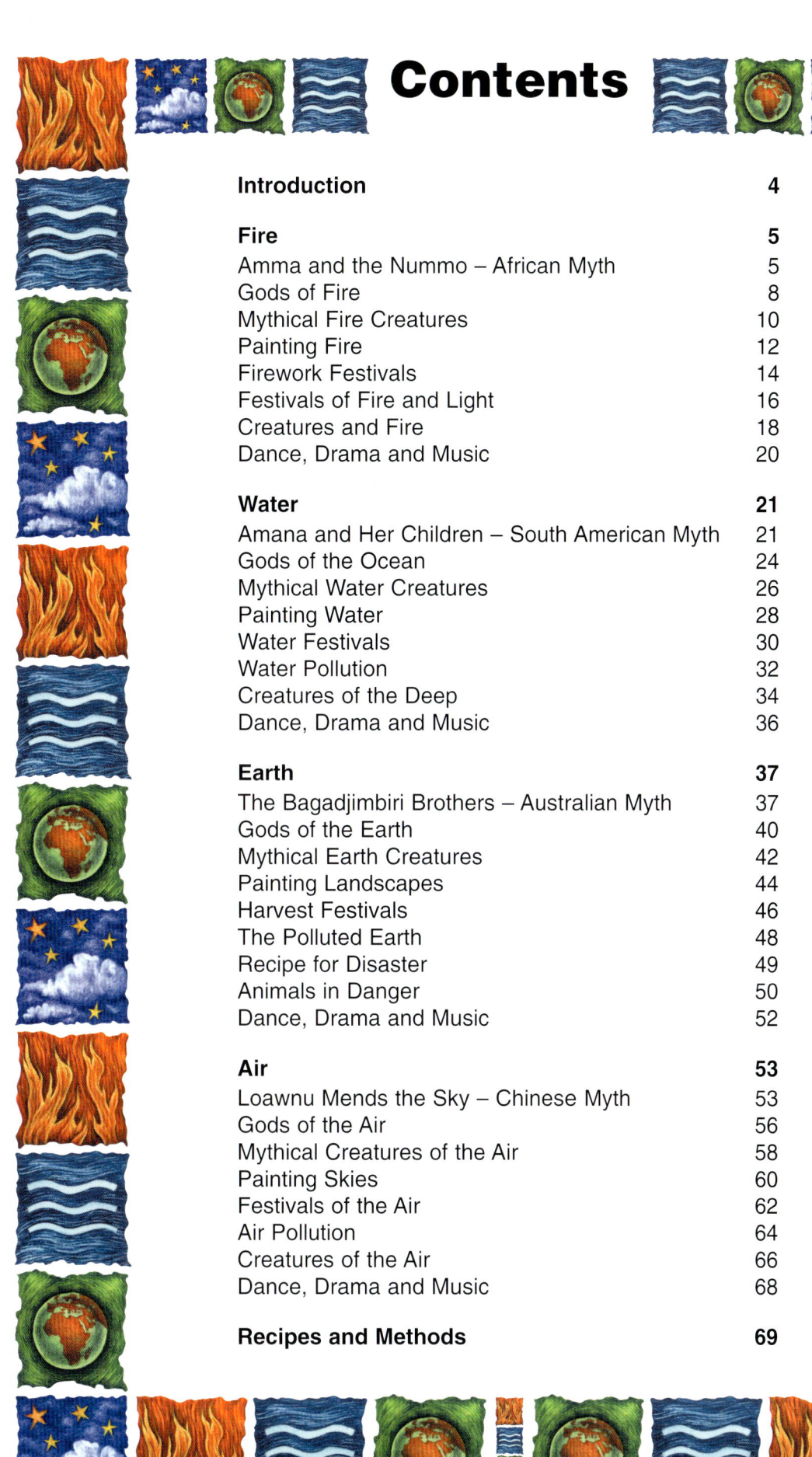

Introduction	4
Fire	**5**
Amma and the Nummo – African Myth	5
Gods of Fire	8
Mythical Fire Creatures	10
Painting Fire	12
Firework Festivals	14
Festivals of Fire and Light	16
Creatures and Fire	18
Dance, Drama and Music	20
Water	**21**
Amana and Her Children – South American Myth	21
Gods of the Ocean	24
Mythical Water Creatures	26
Painting Water	28
Water Festivals	30
Water Pollution	32
Creatures of the Deep	34
Dance, Drama and Music	36
Earth	**37**
The Bagadjimbiri Brothers – Australian Myth	37
Gods of the Earth	40
Mythical Earth Creatures	42
Painting Landscapes	44
Harvest Festivals	46
The Polluted Earth	48
Recipe for Disaster	49
Animals in Danger	50
Dance, Drama and Music	52
Air	**53**
Loawnu Mends the Sky – Chinese Myth	53
Gods of the Air	56
Mythical Creatures of the Air	58
Painting Skies	60
Festivals of the Air	62
Air Pollution	64
Creatures of the Air	66
Dance, Drama and Music	68
Recipes and Methods	69

Introduction

According to a Hopi Native American legend, worlds have existed before this one but they have been destroyed in turn by different disasters. The first world was destroyed by fire and the second came to an end when the Earth toppled from its axis and everything was covered in fire and ice. The third world was destroyed by a great flood. We now inhabit the fourth world, and its fate – whether it is destroyed by fire, water, earth or air – rests in our hands.

This book offers stories about the four elements: fire, water, earth and air. There are creation myths told by different peoples from various countries around the world, poems about mythical creatures, descriptions of festivals connected with the four elements and many other imaginative ideas to stimulate your children's creativity through writing, poetry, drama, dance, music and art. Environmental issues feature strongly in the book as it is only through an understanding of how pollution is changing our world that children can appreciate how vital the elements are to human life and how children have the power to change things in the future. I hope that some of the magic of the elements can reach and inspire your children through this book.

Valerie Evans

Fire

Amma and the Nummo – African Myth

Everything was dark apart from a reddish glow coming from Amma's forge in the smithy that he had built in heaven. Amma took some clay and made two balls which he put into the fire of the forge. The largest ball he threw into the sky to be the Sun. The smaller ball was thrown into the sky to be the Moon. Amma used the clay that was left to make hundreds of stars to light up the sky. Next, Amma modelled a clay woman as Earth. He breathed life into her and then married her because he was lonely. Earth soon found that she was expecting their first child. Amma and Earth were very excited but a great shock was in store for them. Earth gave birth to a Jackal who was not kind and loving as they had hoped – he was a very wicked, mischievous creature. Jackal did not live with his parents in heaven, he wandered around on the Earth, waiting for a chance to cause trouble.

Amma and Earth decided to have another child, but this time they were blessed with twins – one boy and one girl – who became known as the Nummo. Although the top halves of their bodies were human, instead of walking on legs they wriggled around on the bodies of serpents, which were covered with sparkling green hair. Their eyes burned with the colours of fire. Amma decided that the twins should make the first people to live on the Earth. He wanted them to make plants, birds and animals but he warned them that the new people on Earth should not have fire. Amma was the maker of fire and he did not want humans to have his power. The Nummo followed their father's instructions. They drew a male and a female on the ground and breathed life into them. This couple had many children, all of whom were twins.

One of the sons was called Serau. He lived in heaven where he grew to manhood. Then he married and had his own family and he asked the Nummo if he could travel to Earth and settle there. Serau wanted to be a farmer on Earth and grow crops, but he dearly wished to take fire with him. The Nummo were concerned that the Jackal was still on Earth where he could do harm, so Serau was told that the Earth was not yet finished and he must wait. But Serau was not prepared to wait any longer, and he planned his escape.

Serau didn't want to escape to Earth without his family, so he made a large clay granary to hide them in. After stealing fire from Amma's forge, which he put into bellows, he escaped down the rainbow that joins heaven to Earth. The Nummo tried to stop him by shouting and throwing thunder and lightning at him. The bolts of lightning hit Serau and, as he fell, people, plants, flowers, birds and animals fell to Earth with him. This was the beginning of human life on Earth but it was a bad start. People were influenced by the thoughts and deeds of the Jackal. He taught them anger, hate, distrust and fear. One man fought another and they were unable to live in peace because Serau had gone to Earth before it was ready.

a creation myth, told by the Dogon people of Mali

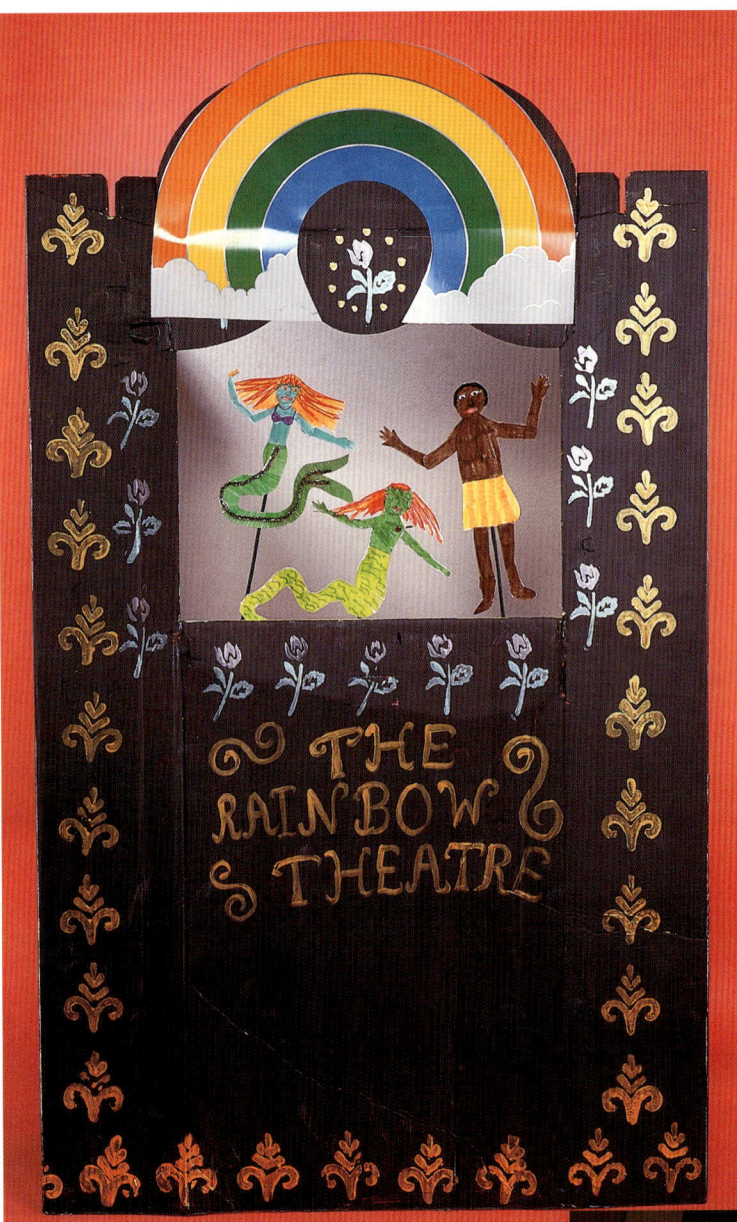

- 'Amma and the Nummo' is a creation myth, told by the Dogon people of Mali. Find out where Mali is on a globe or map.

- Amma used clay to make the Sun, Moon and hundreds of stars. Find out where clay comes from and explore how to model with it. Compare fired and unfired clay, and discuss why Amma put the clay into the fire of the forge.

- Use clay to model suns, moons and stars. Use a pencil or a clay tool to make a hole in the models for hanging. Paint with bronze, silver and gold paints.

- Find compound words beginning with 'sun' and 'moon', for example sunshine, sunburn, sundial, moonlight, moonbeam, moonraker. Write them on sun and moon shapes.

- Jackal was described in the story as 'a very wicked, mischievous creature'. Make a list of adjectives to describe Amma, the Nummo and Serau.

- List possible reasons why Amma did not want humans to have fire, and why Serau was so keen to take fire with him that he stole it.

- Write a playscript based on the story of 'Amma and the Nummo', using the characters of Amma, his wife Earth, the Jackal, the Nummo and Serau.

- Make shadow puppets to enact the playscripts. Cut out strong body outlines and attach green gardening sticks to the back of the puppets with masking tape so that they can be made to move easily.

- Make a large cardboard puppet theatre. Decorate it using stencils to paint on designs or printing blocks to print a pattern. Make background scenery for the play.

- Design programmes which include a short introduction to the play.

- Rewrite the story of 'Amma and the Nummo' from a particular character's point of view, for example, Earth's, Serau's or the Jackal's.

- Write an escape plan for Serau and his family. Think about how and when he would travel to Earth and what he would take with him.

- Illustrate Serau's escape from Heaven in the form of a mobile. Cover a coat-hanger with 'the rainbow that joins Heaven to Earth' and suspend Serau and all the items that fell to Earth on different lengths of string or wool.

- The Nummo were half human and half serpent. Find out about other mythical creatures that are half human and half animal, such as the centaur in Greek mythology which was half man and half horse, and the Egyptian sphinx which had a human head and a lion's body. Invent new creatures that are half human and half animal and think of names for these creations.

- Find out the meaning of the following words from the story: 'forge', 'smithy', 'granary' and 'bellows'. Draw an illustration for each word.

- Jackal wandered around on Earth waiting for a chance to cause trouble. He taught human beings to feel anger, hate, distrust and fear. Make up a story about one of Jackal's mischievous deeds that taught one of these negative emotions to the humans.

Gods of Fire

In early times people thought that fire gods lived inside volcanoes and that eruptions were caused by the gods getting angry about something. Lots of stories were made up about the gods who lived in volcanoes. The Romans said that Vulcan was the blacksmith of the gods. The volcano was believed to be the chimney leading from his forge. When there were explosions from the volcano, people said that Vulcan was hard at work and that the explosions were the sound of Vulcan's hammer on the anvil, and the smoke and flames were from the forge. The island of Vulcano, near Italy, gave its name to all volcanoes, and 23 August was named Vulcan's Day. In Rome, a grand temple was built in his honour.

- Design a card to celebrate Vulcan's Day. Show Vulcan working in his forge inside the volcano.

- Create an erupting volcano using a glass jar, Plasticine, baking soda, red food colouring and vinegar. Build up the Plasticine around the glass jar to resemble a volcano. Half fill the jar with baking soda and add a few drops of red food colouring and some vinegar, one spoon at a time, and watch the volcano erupt.

- Make a fact book about volcanoes. Concertina-fold a rectangular strip of thin card into triangular sections. Illustrate the cover with a volcano, adding pipecleaners and tissue paper to make it look three dimensional. Add appropriate words erupting from the crater, for example 'active', 'dormant', 'erupting' and 'lava'.

- Make a volcano batik using melted wax crayons. Draw a volcano in pencil on thick, white cotton material. Melt pieces of wax crayon and paint the designs different colours. Leave it to dry and then roll the material into a tight ball to crack the wax. Iron between sheets of clean sugar paper.

- Vulcan was just one of the Roman gods. Find out about the other gods that were so important in the everyday lives of the Romans.

⚠ **Note:** The children should be closely supervised when working with hot wax.

The people of Hawaii believed in a fire goddess called Pele. Pele went from island to island, searching for one that she liked enough to live on. She tried several islands and built volcanoes on them before deciding not to stay. Eventually, she reached Kilauea on the island of Hawaii and made her home there. Many people claim to have seen her just before an eruption and say that she and her family are dancing when a volcano erupts. Others say that when she gets angry molten lava pours from her head and turns people and animals into stone. A strange form of lava is thrown out when the Kilauea volcano erupts and because it looks like hair it is called 'Pele's hair'. Birds use it for building their nests.

- Look at a world map that shows the locations of volcanoes. Find Kilauea on the island of Hawaii and look for other volcanic islands that Pele might have visited.

- Paint a picture of Pele and her family dancing during an eruption. Use red, orange and yellow marbling inks to make a marbled flame background and then add black silhouettes for the dancing figures.

- Paint a volcano, then pour runny paint onto the paper around the crater. Blow the paint from above with a straw. When this has dried, use felt-tipped pens to make the shape into Pele's face, with lava pouring from her head.

- Paint a large volcano on a piece of folded card so that it opens to reveal the inner parts. Clearly label the main parts (crater, main pipe, magma chamber and Earth's crust). Glue glitter pipecleaners and curled strips of paper around the crater. Display Pele and her family erupting from the volcano as a background.

- Write an imaginative story or myth to explain why volcanoes erupt.

- Many people believed that lava poured from Pele's head and turned people and animals into stone. Use information sources to find out about the nature of volcanic eruptions and provide a logical explanation for their beliefs. Discuss why such beliefs evolved.

Mythical Fire Creatures

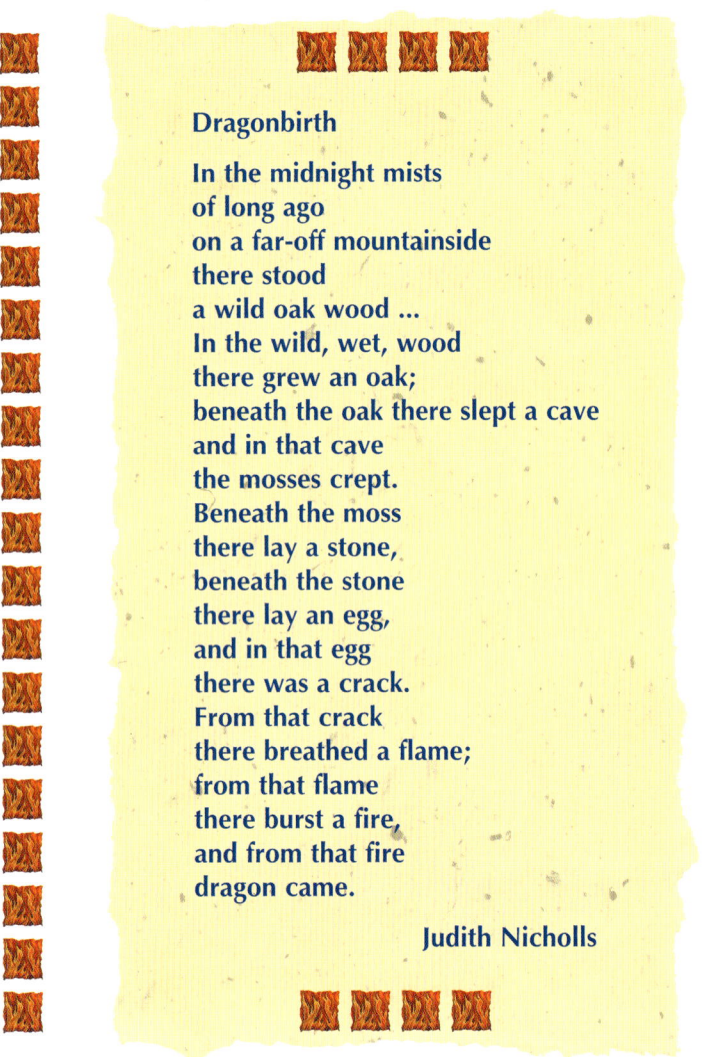

Dragonbirth

In the midnight mists
of long ago
on a far-off mountainside
there stood
a wild oak wood ...
In the wild, wet, wood
there grew an oak;
beneath the oak there slept a cave
and in that cave
the mosses crept.
Beneath the moss
there lay a stone,
beneath the stone
there lay an egg,
and in that egg
there was a crack.
From that crack
there breathed a flame;
from that flame
there burst a fire,
and from that fire
dragon came.

Judith Nicholls

- Read 'Dragonbirth' and identify how the use of descriptive language creates the mood and builds tension. How effective is the use of repetition in the poem in creating an atmosphere?

- The poet uses alliteration in her description of the wood – 'In the wild, wet, wood'. Think of alliterative phrases to describe the mist, the oak, the cave, the egg and the fire.

- Illustrate the poem 'Dragonbirth' using water-soluble pencils. Draw a landscape of mountains and trees on paper cut to an oval shape to represent the egg. Add a prominent oak tree and a cave in the foreground and show the dragon emerging from a cracked egg. Apply the colours dry and then use a soft brush dipped in water to blend the colours for an atmospheric effect.

- In the poem 'Dragonbirth', the dragon is born and emerges from a burst of fire. Find out about other mythical creatures that can live in fire and remain unharmed, such as the phoenix and the fire salamander.

- Create your own fire creatures that emerge from the flames of a fire and write poems about them in the same style as 'Dragonbirth'. Write the poems on painted card flames.

- Imagine witnessing the birth of the dragon on the mountainside, in the wild, wet, wood. Write a report describing the event.

- Cinquains have a standard syllable pattern. Each cinquain has five lines, and a total of 22 syllables split into the pattern of 2, 4, 6, 8, 2. Write a cinquain inspired by the poem 'Dragonbirth'. Examples:

Hatching
Egg cracks open
Dragonbirth is complete
Flickering flames burst from the fire
New born.

New dawn
In wild, wet, wood
A large egg slowly splits
Emerging from the red flames comes
Dragon.

The phoenix was an extraordinary bird that lived for a thousand years. When it came to the time for it to die the sun's rays set fire to its funeral pyre and a new phoenix would rise from the ashes. As a phoenix was only born every thousand years it was not an event that many people would have witnessed.

- Write a newspaper report under one of the following headlines: 'Extraordinary Bird Rises from the Ashes', 'Phoenix Symbolises New Hope for the World' or 'Was it Worth the Wait?'

- Imagine a phoenix. Draw the mythical firebird on thin card and then dribble PVA glue along the outline. Leave to dry and harden overnight, then spray or brush on gold or silver paint. When the paint is dry, rub over the picture with black shoe polish and finally red shoe polish to highlight the flames.

- Make a concertina booklet with seven pages, one for each letter in the word 'phoenix'. On the first page draw a phoenix for the letter 'p', then invent mythical firebirds and beasts for the remaining letters.

Painting Fire

The Burning of the Houses of Parliament by William Turner (1775–1851) is an exciting and dramatic painting to study. Look at different examples of Turner's work to show how he loved the effect of steam, smoke or mist swirling around his landscapes. *The Burning of the Houses of Parliament* will demonstrate how a dramatic fire can be painted realistically and it may lead to work on reflections in water as the flames are reflected here in the river Thames.

- Use pastels to work in the style of Turner. Draw a burning bridge or a forest inferno. Make the work as atmospheric as possible by smudging and blending the pastels with the fingers.

- Turner's painting shows the Houses of Parliament, London, in flames. Choose another famous building, such as the Empire State Building, Sydney Opera House or the Eiffel Tower, and paint it on fire, copying Turner's atmospheric style. Give the work a title.

- In Turner's painting the fire is reflected in the river Thames. Paint a burning building beside water. If the water is still, the reflection will be a clear mirror image. If the water is fast-running, the reflection will be broken up and imperfect.

- Try painting a fire with watercolour paints. First, paint a background with yellow, orange and red paints. Next, while the paint is still wet, splatter the work with clean water so that the colours run and blur. When this has dried, add buildings, animals or trees to the fire scene.

- Paint a piece of white paper with a solution of water and icing sugar. While the paper is still wet, paint on a fire scene and watch the way the colours blend and blur. When the painting has dried it will have an interesting grainy effect.

- Finger-painting can produce some interesting fiery effects. Smear yellow and red paint onto paper to create flames. Make orange shades by mixing yellows and reds together. Use finger-painting to paint bonfires or volcanoes spitting out flames and ash. Grey swirls of smoke will add to the final effect.

- Blow-painting works very successfully in fire pictures. Mix red and yellow paints with water until runny and then pour them onto a sheet of paper a little at a time. Blow through a straw over the paint to make flame shapes.

- To paint fireworks use the painting *Falling Rocket* by James McNeill Whistler for inspiration. This was painted in 1874 and was inspired by a firework display in a London park. Demonstrate how to splatter paint with a toothbrush to create a firework effect.

- Make printing blocks in the shape of fireworks by gluing string, sponge, pipecleaners or pasta onto a piece of wood or stiff cardboard. Paint the fireworks with fluorescent paint and print onto black paper.

Firework Festivals

Fireworks were invented by the Chinese over 2000 years ago. Today they are used at different celebrations around the world. In France, they are used to celebrate Bastille Day each July, recalling how the Paris crowds stormed the Bastille prison and gained independence. In Britain, fireworks are lit each year on 5 November to remember Guy Fawkes' attempt to blow up the Houses of Parliament in 1605. In the United States, on 4 July, fireworks are used to celebrate American Independence Day. In China, fireworks are let off to celebrate the New Year.

- Write about a world celebration or festival that involves fireworks. Put up a world map in the classroom and display rockets pointing to the country written about.

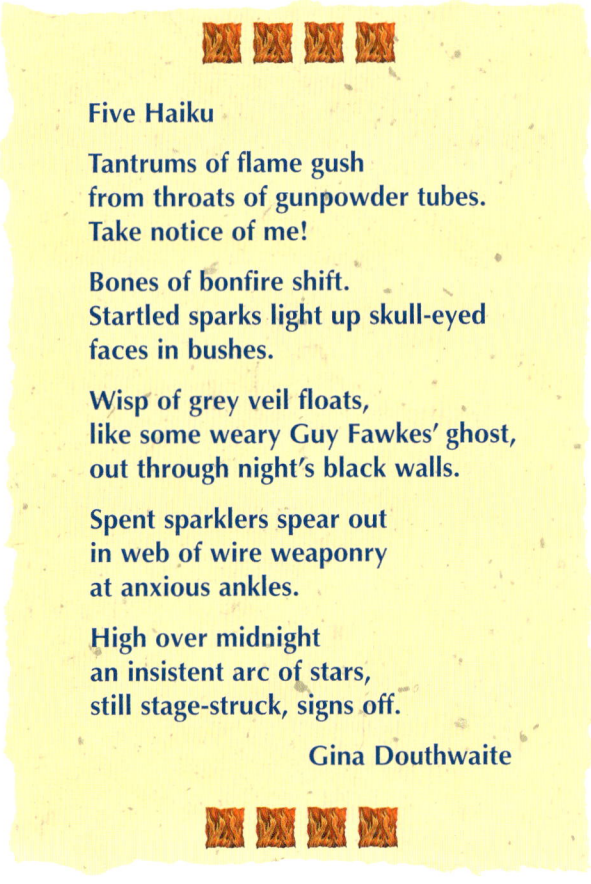

Five Haiku

Tantrums of flame gush
from throats of gunpowder tubes.
Take notice of me!

Bones of bonfire shift.
Startled sparks light up skull-eyed
faces in bushes.

Wisp of grey veil floats,
like some weary Guy Fawkes' ghost,
out through night's black walls.

Spent sparklers spear out
in web of wire weaponry
at anxious ankles.

High over midnight
an insistent arc of stars,
still stage-struck, signs off.

Gina Douthwaite

- Read 'Five Haiku' by Gina Douthwaite. Identify the metaphorical use of language in the poem, for example 'Tantrums of flame', 'Bones of bonfire'. With what do you associate her descriptions?

- In the fourth verse of 'Five Haiku', Gina Douthwaite makes good use of alliteration: 'Spent sparklers spear out', 'in web of wire weaponry'. Make up some more alliterative firework phrases, for example 'spitting sparklers spun in spirals'.

- Haiku are short Japanese poems of 3 lines and 17 syllables, 5 in the first line, 7 in the second and 5 in the third (a 5–7–5 pattern). Make up some more haiku to describe fireworks being let off at a special celebration.

- Does the poem 'Five Haiku' succeed in helping you imagine the atmosphere, sounds, sights and smells of bonfire night? Write about a firework festival that you have been to.

- Write firework shape-poems in the shape of rockets, sparklers and Catherine wheels.

- What noises do fireworks make? 'Whee', 'whoosh', 'zizzzz-phhht', 'pow' – a great time for onomatopoeia! Add some of these sounds to a firework collage. The writing can be done in glue and sprinkled with glitter. Foil and fluorescent paints will add to the overall effect.

- Make fireworks from self-hardening clay. Add pieces of wire for the trails of sparks. Paint the fireworks and glue different coloured stars to the trails of wire. Decorate shoe boxes for storing the fireworks!

- Design a new and exciting firework. Describe what it looks like, what happens when it is lit and what noises it makes. Think of a name for the firework.

- Make soft sculpture fireworks from felt, padded with kapok. Add glitter pipe-cleaners, wool or straws as sparks.

- Make a tie-dye background for a firework appliqué. Tie clumps of stones, marbles, shells and coins into the cloth before dying in cold water dye to give some interesting, explosive patterns. (See page 71 for tie-dye methods.)

- Make up a firework safety code. Use the letters in the word 'Fireworks' to begin each new line.

Festivals of Fire and Light

Holi

Holi is the great Hindu festival of spring which is celebrated each year in February or March. Each region of India has its own special way of celebrating Holi. A large communal bonfire is built for the celebrations. After a visit to the temple, holy water is poured onto the bonfire and then it is lit. As the fire burns, people remember the story of Prince Prahlad and the wicked witch Holika which is told to show how good overcomes evil.

Once the bonfire is burning well, people throw popcorn, rice, sweet dates, coconuts and sometimes even money onto the fire. Women walk around the fire praying that their children will have the same health as Krishna did when he was a baby. When the coconuts are pulled from the flames they are allowed to cool down, then they are cracked open so that everyone can eat the white flesh. At the end of the celebration, the ashes of the fire are smeared onto people's foreheads to bring them good luck.

- Tell the story about Prince Prahlad and Holika told in *Hindu Festivals* by Dilip Kadodwala and Paul Gateshill (Heinemann, 1995).

- Act out the story. Choose children to play Prince Prahlad, his father and Holika, and then organise the others into three groups: one group of snakes, one group of elephants and one group to dance like flames.

- Make costumes for the story of Prince Prahlad (elephant masks, fire raffia skirts and fire head-dresses). Decorate socks to wear on the arms as snakes.

- Discuss the importance of hand movements in Indian dance and storytelling. Ask the children to use their hands to mime moods, such as gentleness, excitement and anger.

- What do Hindu people do to bring them good luck and health? What superstitions and symbols of good luck do the children know?

Diwali

Candles are used in many different celebrations, including the Hindu festival of Diwali. The name 'Diwali' comes from *deepawali* which means 'row of lights'. During Diwali, which lasts for five days, people put lamps and candles in their windows. As these are often new lamps, it is a busy time for potters who work in the street using large potters' wheels. The new lamps are thought to help the souls of the dead find their way to heaven. Even the rivers are lit with candles in little paper boats. The god Rama is remembered at Diwali because this is when Indians believe that he rescued his wife Sita and killed the demon Ravana.

- During Diwali, Hindus remember the story of Rama and Sita who returned to their kingdom after fourteen years of exile. They were welcomed home with many lighted lamps. Read the story of 'Rama and Sita' from *Out of the Ark* by Anita Ganeri (Hodder Wayland, 1998).

- The traditional oil lamps lit during Diwali are called diwas. Make a clay lamp, or diwa, by moulding clay around nightlights in the shape of elephants, snakes or small boats. Once dry, they can be painted, varnished and decorated with beads and sequins.

- At Diwali Hindus light lamps to Kali, the Mother Goddess. They believe that if they light lamps for Kali she will rid the world of evil. Write about the bad things in the world that you would like Kali to change.

- At Diwali, rangoli patterns are put on the doorstep to welcome visitors to the house. Design and then chalk rangoli patterns onto the school playground or near each classroom door to welcome other children.

St Lucia

St Lucia is the Swedish Christian saint of light and brightness. On 13 December, to celebrate light and the coming festivities of Christmas, girls dress in white and wear head-dresses of shining candles set in wreaths of evergreen leaves.

- Find out who St Lucia is and why she is a saint.

- Make a St Lucia head-dress with card candles and leaves from evergreen shrubs and trees. How do evergreens differ from deciduous trees? Why will a head-dress made from evergreen leaves be more successful?

- Find out about other celebrations in which candles are part of the festivities.

Creatures and Fire

Walya and Gurigoo
– South American Legend

Deep in the dark jungle, Walya the jaguar wandered around unable to find his way. Walya was friendly with a toad named Kroto who knew the secret of making fire. Kroto found a stick and rubbed it against a piece of wood until it sparked. Walya copied Kroto and he too was able to make fire. When the fire was burning, all Walya's jungle friends arrived to see what was going on. Gurigoo, the Indian boy, came with snake, parrot, toucan, Cotton-top, the tamarin monkey, and quetzal. To celebrate making fire, Walya began to dance round and round the flames but he went much too close and his coat caught fire. He put the fire out by licking his fur, but the fire had burnt black rings on his coat and there they remain to this day.

The other animals thought that Walya looked wonderful in his new coat. Walya picked up one of the burning sticks very carefully with his mouth and carried it home. He had decided to guard fire by day and to use it to light his way at night. Walya loved sitting at the entrance to his cave watching the flames leap and dance and imagining pictures in the shapes of the flames. He watched the rings of colour in the flames until that was all he could see. Walya began to cry, 'I've been burnt by the flames and now I've been blinded by them.' Parrot told Walya to go to the pool of magic water guarded by the red ibises. An ibis dropped some magic water into his eyes and he was able to look around him and see all his friends. The magic water not only helped Walya to see in the day – he could now see in the dark, too. He no longer needed the firelight to see at night.

Walya told Gurigoo, the Indian boy, how to make fire. Gurigoo was delighted with fire as it gave him warmth and he was able to cook his food. Gurigoo cooked a special meal for all his friends and he called Walya when it was ready. But Walya was now afraid that the fire would burn him or make him blind, so he went back to his cave in the dark and alone. Since then, jaguars have always been afraid of fire.

a story to explain why jaguars are afraid of fire, based on legends of the South American peoples

© Belair

- The story tells how the jaguar got its patterned coat by going too close to the fire and getting burnt. Make up a story to explain how the zebra got its stripes, how the parrot got its coloured feathers, how the leopard got its spots or how the tiger got its stripes. Make a frame and decorate with felt-tipped pens or wrapping paper to represent the appropriate patterned fur or feathers.

- Walya had many different animal friends – snake, toad, parrot, toucan, tamarin monkey, quetzal and ibis. Talk about the animals of the Amazon rainforest. Find out what a quetzal and an ibis are. Research and write about one of the animals in the story.

- Write a description of your chosen animal under the heading, 'What am I?'. Write the answer under a flap so that other children can lift the flap to discover which animal has been described. Illustrate the work. (See the photograph on page 2).

- When Walya was blinded, parrot told him to go to the pool of magic water guarded by red ibises. The magic water restored his sight. What other suggestions might the different animals have had for Walya? Think of other items in the jungle that might have had a magical power, such as the juice from an exotic fruit or the nectar from a special flower.

- Walya told Gurigoo, the Indian boy, how to make fire. Gurigoo used fire for warmth and to cook food. Discuss how useful fire has been to humankind. Research and write about the uses of fire today.

- Walya would sit watching the flames leap and dance and imagine pictures in the shape of the flames. Pour runny poster paint onto sugar paper and with a straw blow it into flame shapes. What pictures do the flames suggest? Draw a picture in each flame.

Dance, Drama and Music

Dance

- Brainstorm words connected with fire such as 'flicker', 'blaze', 'writhe' and 'twist'. Write them on cut-out, flame-shaped cards.

- Stand in a large circle and use a flame card to start the fire. The fire begins with a child writhing, for example, beginning with their arms and then spreading to the whole of their body. Link on to the people either side as the fire movements spread. Once everybody is moving you can extinguish the flames.

- Spread the flame cards around the floor. Begin by moving in a way that is described on the card nearest to you. Dance in this way until you meet another card. Change your fire movements according to the card you meet.

- Create a dance to the fire goddess Pele. Work on exploding body shapes in the air, some with soft landings others with loud dramatic landings. Conclude with a dramatic finishing position as if set in stone.

Drama

- Read the story of 'Walya and Gurigoo' (see page 18). Adopt the role of one of the animals in the story. Begin by asking them questions to establish their character, for example: 'Toucan, why do you have such a large and colourful bill?' 'What made you, a bird, become friends with Walya?' Continue in pairs.

- Create a drama in which the animals are trying to convince Walya that his newly burnt coat looks really attractive. Work in groups and ask each group to emphasise one of the following:

  – Reasons why the black rings could be of benefit to Walya in the jungle;

  – Ways to make him realise how attractive the black rings are;

  – Solutions to disguise the black rings.

  Which group can best convince Walya that the rings are either useful or attractive?

Music

- Sitting in a large circle, use only the body and the voice to create the sounds of a fireworks display, for example pzzzzzt, wheeeee, pop, whizz, rubbing hands together, clapping, stamping feet, patting knees and so on. Move around the circle, with each child contributing a noise to the display. Finish with a grand finale in which everyone makes their firework sound together!

Water

Amana and Her Children – South American Myth

Looking up at the star constellation Pleiades, it is hard to imagine a huge blue ocean there, teeming with sea creatures. The sea creatures are similar to those you might find in the Earth's oceans but the seabed is covered with glistening stars instead of sand, and the waves are caused by solar winds. In this magical star ocean there are volcanoes and when one erupts there are beautiful constellation showers.

This ocean in the sky is the home of the sea queen Amana, who is loved by all the sea creatures. Amana is a radiant queen who looks rather like a mermaid but has the longer tail of a sea-serpent. She is followed by shoals of fish and schools of dolphins and many other sea creatures as she glides through the water on the back of a large, old turtle.

All was well while Amana and the sea life were the only living creatures in the universe, but things began to go wrong when the volcanoes erupted and tossed planets into a sky that had been completely empty apart from the Sun. Amana couldn't bear to look at these bleak, empty planets around her. She began covering them with trees, plants and flowers. She added sea creatures, and clouds to shade the scorching sun.

Amana was very pleased with her creations, but the Sun was far from happy. He had been Amana's first creation and he was jealous of the new stars and planets, so he scorched the life on as many planets as he could and sent fire-serpents to swallow Amana's ocean. Luckily, the ocean waves put out the flames but Amana was fearful of what the Sun would try next.

Amana needed bodyguards to protect her kingdom so she gave birth to two boys, both on the same day. The first boy was born in the morning when it was pleasantly cool and the second was born in the evening after the Sun had gone down. Her boys were opposites in every way. Amana called her morning son Tamusi and her evening son Tamulu. Tamusi was lord of light but it was a cold, icy light. When the fire-serpents attacked again, Tamusi sliced them into little pieces with his icy light and their remains were scattered into the air. Tamulu was the lord of darkness and by night he and his goblins caught and killed any remaining fire-serpents. Eventually the brothers brought an end to the Sun's attacks and Amana was able to turn her attention to creating human life on Earth.

Amana chose Tamusi to design the people who would inhabit the Earth. After drawing lots of sketches he finally settled on creatures that had upper bodies with a head and arms like his mother but two legs below to move on. When these people were put on the Earth Tamulu looked down in anger. He had wanted to create the first people. To cause trouble Tamulu created phantoms and monsters which still roam the Earth as darkness falls. When daylight comes the human race is safe again in Tamusi's hands.

a creation myth, told by the Calina people of South America

- The story of 'Amana and Her Children' is a creation myth, told by the Calina people of South America. Find South America in an atlas or on a globe.

- Talk about what a creation myth is and find other creation stories to share. Write your own creation myth about how the world began.

- Early people noticed that stars are clustered together in groups, forming different shapes. They called these 'constellations', meaning groups of stars, and gave them names. Use reference sources to find out more about stars. Draw and name some of the constellations.

- Design and name a new constellation of your own.

- The story tells how Amana is loved by all the sea creatures around her. Make a list of different sea creatures. Pick a creature from the list and vividly describe it for others to guess what it is.

- Tamusi sketched the first people who would live on Earth. Make sketches of a creature that is half human and half sea creature, for example a creature with a woman's body and eight octopus legs, or the head and body of a seahorse and the legs of a man. Write a description of your creature.

- Write a plan of destruction for the Sun. Explain how it could destroy Amana's work. Discuss what jealousy feels like and if they are happy with revenge. Display the writing on brightly painted suns.

- Highlight the adjectives used in the story to describe the constellation showers, the ocean, the queen, the turtle and the planets. Think of two alternative adjectives to describe each noun, for example the 'enormous ancient turtle' instead of the 'large old turtle'.

- Discuss the term 'collective noun' and find examples in the story. Make up your own collective nouns for octopuses, turtles, sea-serpents and starfish.

- Make a collage of dough sea creatures telling a part of the story of 'Amana and Her Children' (see page 69 for dough recipe). Make lots of stars to cover the seabed. Use a garlic press to make Amana's hair and the tentacles of jellyfish. Use a potato masher to decorate the turtles' shells.

- Make a list of verbs used in the story (cover, erupt, love, look, glide, toss, like, add, scorch, etc.). Experiment by replacing each verb with a synonym or antonym and discuss the impact on the meaning of the story.

- Amana did not like the bleak and empty planets around her. Design a planet for Amana. What plants, trees, flowers and animals would you put on this completely empty planet? Give your planet a name.

- Tamulu and Tamusi were opposite in every way. Write out a list of opposites to describe both of Amana's sons.

- Tamulu created phantoms and monsters to roam the Earth and cause trouble when darkness fell. Describe some of the tricks and pranks that these monsters may have played on the first humans.

- In the story of 'Amana and Her Children' the feelings of love, contentment, jealousy, anger and spite all feature. Write about your own experience or make up a story based on one of these emotions.

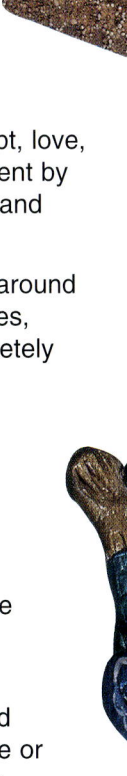

Gods of the Ocean

Poseidon was Lord of the ocean. He rode the seas in a chariot drawn by strange animals, half horse and half sea-serpent. His symbols included a trident for controlling the seas, a bull to represent his aggression and a horse (he was supposed to have created the first horse). Poseidon was believed to have made storms, caused floods, completely dried up rivers and split open the Earth.

- Poseidon used his trident to control the seas. Find out what a trident is. Think of other words that begin with 'tri' and make a list (examples: triangle, tricycle, tripod, tricolour, triplets).

- Ask the children to imagine that they are an undersea god with a magic trident and to write a story about an adventure in which they controlled the waters.

- Design and make a shield for Poseidon which includes his symbols: a trident, a bull and a horse.

- The Ancient Greeks believed that Poseidon built a city of golden palaces called Atlantis. They believed that a flood destroyed the legendary city and that its remains lie somewhere at the bottom of the ocean. Use boxes and corrugated card to make the city of Atlantis. Add shells and spray with gold paint.

- Poseidon is an ancestor of some of the fiercest creatures in Greek mythology – the Hydra, Sphinx, Echidna and Cerberus. Use reference sources to find out about these awesome monsters.

Ancient Romans believed Neptune ruled the sea with the help of his wife Amphitrite and his son Triton, who played the part of his herald. Triton was a demi-god, and was half man and half fish. Neptune rode over the sea in his chariot drawn by horses, while Amphitrite rode in a shell with Nereides as her attendants. Nereides were beautiful girls with pearls in their hair who rode on the backs of dolphins.

- Draw a family portrait of Neptune clothed in seaweed holding his trident, with Amphitrite sitting in her shell and his son Triton, half man and half fish.

- Design a different form of transport suitable for Neptune's son Triton.

- Ancient Roman villas had gardens decorated with fountains and statues of gods, people or animals. Design a garden for a large villa and include an ornamental fountain with a statue of Neptune. What other features would you use to decorate your garden?

- The Romans used tiny coloured tiles to make decorative patterns, called mosaics, on their floors. Using small squares cut from different coloured sticky-backed plastic, design a mosaic showing Neptune controlling the seas.

- Read Judith Nicholls' poem 'Put on your Thinking Hat!' Can the children attempt to answer the questions posed by the poem?

- Design either an underwater thinking hat or a dreaming hat. Give the children a varied selection of collage materials to make their oceanic headgear. (See photograph on page 36.)

- Ask the children to write their own two-verse poems beginning 'Put on your thinking hat and tell me ...' Ask three questions in each verse.

- Make a seascape box for displaying each poem. Cut out a sandpaper frame to fit over the top of a tissue box. Glue to the box and decorate with shells and pebbles. Write the poem on bluey-green paper and stick it on the box, inside the sandpaper frame.

Put on your Thinking Hat!

Put on your thinking hat and tell me ...
Who is king of the seas?
And how does an angel-fish fly?
Why are there caves in the ocean,
　　... tell me why?

Put on your dreaming hat and tell me ...
Is his crown made of seaweed and pearl?
Do sea-horses wait on him there?
And where is his throne in the coral,
　　... tell me where?

　　　　　　　　　Judith Nicholls

- Make up a list of ten questions about gods or creatures of the ocean. Talk about the way we begin and end questions. Ask the children to give their list of ten questions to a partner who then has to find out the answers.

- Angel-fish, pearls, coral and sea horses are all mentioned in the poem. Find out facts about coral; is it a plant or animal? Discover how pearls are formed or research the life of a sea horse or angel-fish. Make small zigzag books with four pages giving the facts and information.

Mythical Water Creatures

Mermaids (women to the waist and fish from the waist down) are the most well-known mythical sea creatures. Sailors whose ships ran into rocks would often blame the beautiful mermaids who they claimed had distracted them. Some people believe in these beautiful creatures; other people think that the mermaid myth comes from mistaking the identity of the dugong, a sea mammal that suckles its young in an upright position.

Ten Mermaids

Ten mermaids basking in the sun
Nine mermaids just having fun.
Eight mermaids diving from the rocks
Seven mermaids combing golden locks.
Six mermaids hiding in the caves
Five mermaids surfing in the waves.
Four mermaids eating ice-cream
Three mermaids don't want to be seen.
Two mermaids catching fish
One mermaid making a wish.

— Valerie Evans

- Read the poem 'Ten Mermaids' and identify the rhyme pattern used. Write your own poem using the same format – starting with ten mermaids and working down to one.

- Cut out a scallop shell-shape from folded white card. Glue string along the top to make ridges and cover with small pieces of coloured tissue paper. Display the 'Ten Mermaids' poems in the open shells.

- Make a mermaid chain from folded paper. Fold the paper into sections, one for each mermaid, then outline the mermaids so that their hands and tail-fins touch the folded sides. Cut out the shapes and unfold. Paint the tails with gold or silver, add sequins and use paint or wool for the mermaids' hair. Display with the 'Ten Mermaids' poems.

- Collect words associated with mermaids and the sea. Write these on shell-shaped cards and use as a word bank for writing mermaid poems.

- Imagine that you are a lone fisherman and you see a mermaid. Write an account of this strange sighting, describing your feelings on seeing this beautiful creature.

- Make a tie-dye underwater collage with black felt silhouettes of mermaids, fish, turtles and shells (see page 71). Display as a large underwater banner.

- Liven up a blank wall with a sea mural. Draw the design in pencil, then paint using acrylic paints. When dry, paint over the finished design with acrylic varnish.

- The dugong, also known as a sea-cow, is a sea mammal. Find information about the dugong and other sea mammals using encyclopedias, information books and the internet.

- In Scotland, many people believe in a monster, affectionately called Nessie, who lives in Loch Ness. Find out about some of the supposed sightings of Nessie. Do you think there really is a Loch Ness monster?

- Imagine camping out by Loch Ness for a week, with only a diary and camera with you. You notice several movements in the loch during the week, followed by a sighting of the monster! Record your daily observations and feelings in the diary. Include sketches of the monster.

- Norse legend tells of the kraken, an octopus-like sea monster that was said to overturn fishing boats and large ships. It was over 20 metres long, with thick tentacles and rows of claws for gripping its prey. Its mouth was like a huge beak capable of piercing the side of a ship. Imagine that you were in a boat that managed to escape from the kraken. Draw and describe the monster and write about your experience.

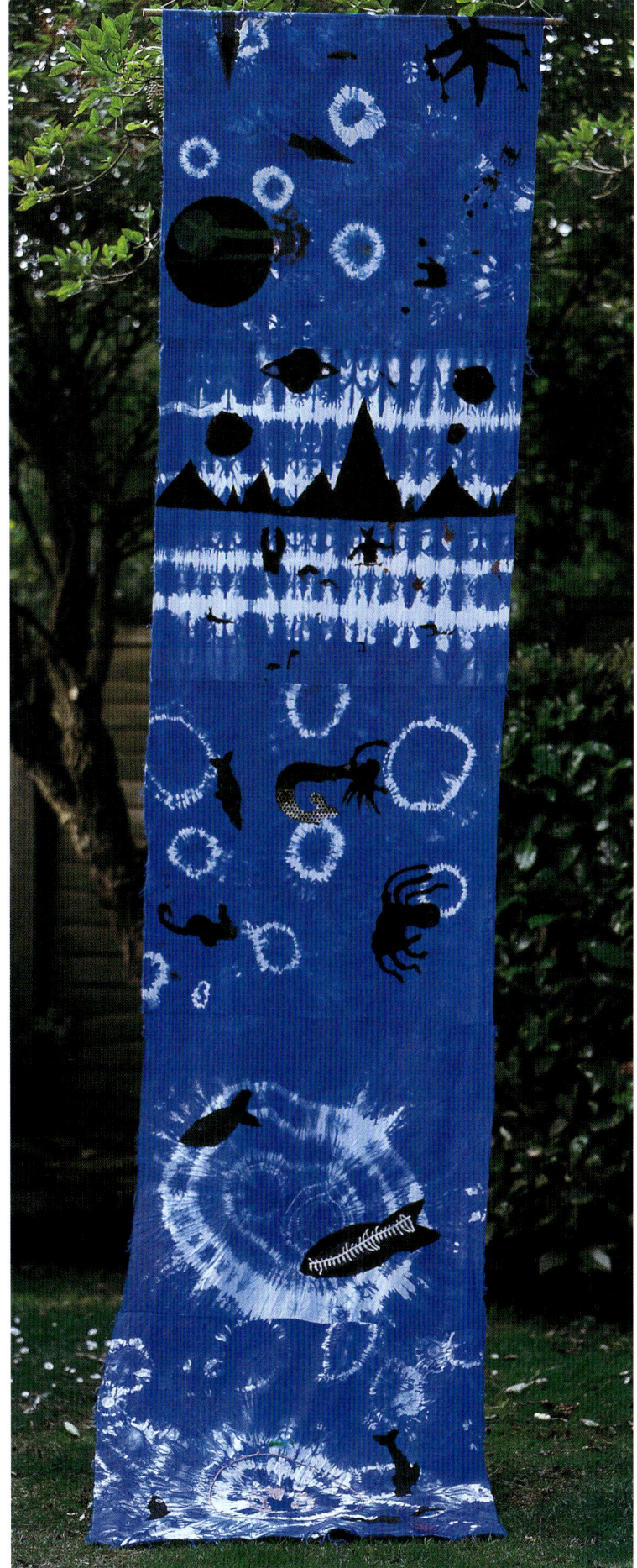

Painting Water

Gustave Courbet (1819–77), a self-taught artist, painted portraits, still lifes, hunting scenes and seascapes. He influenced the rise of Realism, a movement in which artists looked at and represented 'real and existing things'. He rejected the imaginativeness of the Romantic movement, feeling that the artist should paint a historical record of what he or she actually saw.

- Look at Gustave Courbet's *The Wave,* painted c.1871. Talk about the atmospheric quality of the painting, the similarity of colours used for the sea and sky, and how Courbet has emphasised the power of the wave.
- Discuss the techniques Courbet used in his painting to capture a very rough sea. Talk about the colours and textures that the children could use to create their own stormy scene. Scrunched-up greaseproof paper dipped into white paint could be used to print waves onto a background of sky, sea and cliffs. Flick paint from a toothbrush to represent sea spray.
- Use a small sponge for painting the sea to achieve a mottled effect. Use scrunched-up kitchen paper for the waves.
- Draw waves and ripples with white wax crayon, pressing down hard. Paint a blue colour wash on top for a resist effect.
- Paint waterfalls with water cascading over rocks and use scrunched-up paper or kitchen towel to print the spray.

- Look at Hokusai's painting *Off Kanagwa Hollow of a Wave* which is rather stylised and decorative. Compare this with Courbet's Realist painting *The Wave*. Try to paint waves in the style of Hokusai.

- Paint calm seas using long, straight brushstrokes. Alternatively, use chalks or pastels, holding them on their sides and pressing firmly to produce the same long, straight strokes. Add details for extra interest, such as boats, seabirds and a lighthouse.

Water is one of David Hockney's favourite themes and he is particularly fond of painting swimming pools.

- Look at a selection of Hockney's paintings, including *Afternoon Swimming*, and *Picture of a Hollywood Swimming Pool*. Try, like Hockney, to capture the movement of water. Paint in a more abstract way, concentrating on the patterns in the water of the swimming pool.

Water Festivals

Each religion has its own rituals and festivals, many of them involving water. Water is a symbol of cleanliness and goodness. The beginning of a Christian person's life is marked by being baptised with water. For Anglicans, this occurs during a christening ceremony in a church, for which the baby is usually dressed in white – a symbol of cleanliness and purity. At the ceremony, water from the font is blessed by the vicar, scooped up in a shell and poured three times onto the baby's head. The baby is baptised in the name of the Holy Trinity and the sign of a cross is made on his or her forehead.

- Ask if anyone has been to a baptism or christening. Can they bring in photographs for the others to see?
- The child is baptised in the name of the Holy Trinity – what does this mean?
- At a christening, parents and godparents make promises on behalf of the child. What are the promises? Think of three good promises that a Christian might make for a baby.
- How do parents choose a child's name? Do you know why your name was chosen? You may have been named after a relative. Find out what the names of some of your family and friends mean.
- The font is found near the door in many churches. Where would you find the altar, pulpit, pews and lectern? What are they used for?

Water is important in the celebration of Holi, a Hindu festival. Stories explain how the festival of Holi began. Krishna was happily playing his flute and his friends were dancing by the river. When Krishna saw a beautiful girl called Radha he playfully threw some coloured water at her. Ever since then Indian people have celebrated Holi by throwing powder paint and water at each other. At Holi, water is represented on the special Hindu worship tray called an arti. The elements of earth and fire are represented by flowers and incense; light and air are represented by waving a fan.

- Use a thick brush to paint water over a sheet of black or white paper. While it is still wet, splatter with different coloured powder paints. The paint can be sprinkled on with a tablespoon or thrown on. Experiment to see how many different effects you can achieve. Display with writing about the festival of Holi.
- At Holi the element of air is represented by waving a fan. Use wax crayons to make Indian designs on card, pressing down hard to give strong colours. Cover the design with a colourwash made with very watery poster paint. Concertina-fold the card into a fan shape and staple one end. Display with an arti tray, flowers and incense.

'Well-dressing' is a tradition in Derbyshire, England, where there are many springs and streams. Special thanksgiving services are held in many of the churches in the summer months and the wells are 'dressed' the week before the service. The dressing is made entirely from flower petals, greenery, berries and mosses stuck into wet clay. Each well-dressing honours the patron saint of the village church.

- Patron saints are thought to look after a particular group of people, a profession or a country. Each saint has his or her own special festival celebrated every year. Ask the children to find out more about a patron saint of their choice.

- Research the old tradition of well-dressing and make a well-dressing plaque. Roll a slab of self-hardening clay into a rectangle and embed pressed flowers, leaves, shells and small pebbles into the clay to create an interesting design.

More than 2000 years ago a Chinese poet named Ch'u Yuan objected to the way the emperor treated the ordinary people. To make his point to the emperor, Ch'u Yuan threw himself into the river. People jumped into their dragon boats and rushed to rescue him but they did not get there in time to save him. This event is still remembered each year in May or June when dragon boat races are held to remember the race to save Ch'u Yuan's life. A drum beat helps the rowers to keep their rhythm in their beautifully decorated dragon boats.

- Dragon boats are long, slim rowing boats with a dragon's head at one end. Design and make a card model of a dragon boat. Make twelve oars for the boat using gardening sticks and cardboard. Add decorations to the boat using felt-tipped pens or three-dimensional paint squeezed directly from the tube for a raised effect.

- Research other boating festivals held in different countries around the world.

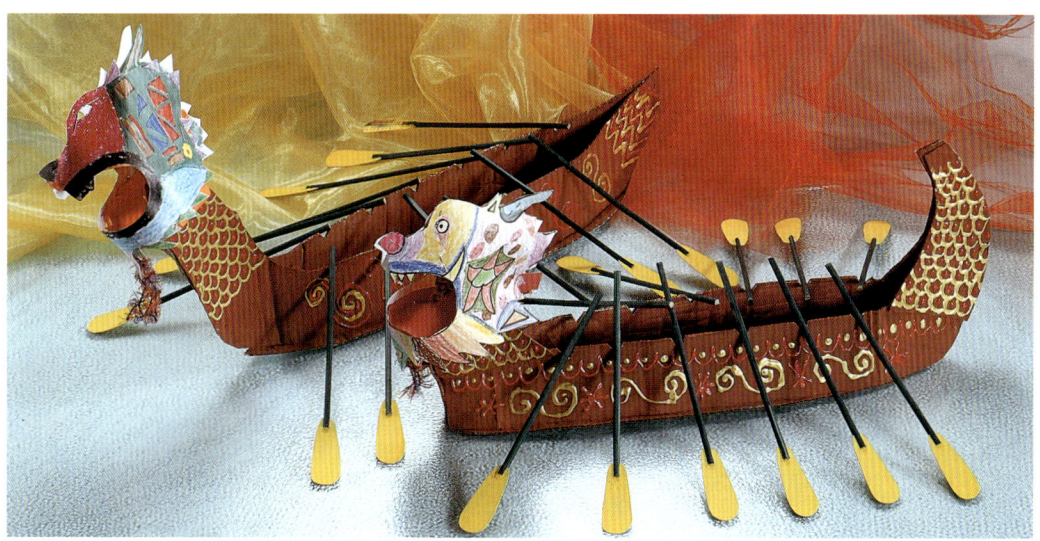

31

Water Pollution

Jetsam

Foaming wave, aftershave
Plastic comb, brittle bone
Bottle top, building block
Wooden spar, plastic car
Thermos top, can of pop
Salt-stained shoe, tin of glue.
Tennis racquet, empty packet
Car tyre, coil of wire
Pram wheel, rubber seal
Tar-blacked stone, fir cone
Rusty lid, twisted grid
Chipboard, orange cord
Empty and faded
Bottle of bleach
Almost forgotten
On a winter beach.

Nigel Cox

- Read the poem 'Jetsam'. What issue does it address? Identify the rhyme pattern used in the poem.

- Find out what the title 'Jetsam' means. Why do the children think the poet chose this as a title for his poem?

- Look at the types of rubbish that are listed in the poem. Consider who might have left each type of rubbish on the beach and why. Do you think it was left by mistake, washed ashore or dumped?

- List the items of rubbish in the poem that will rot, go rusty or fade. Talk about biodegradable materials. What does this term mean?

- The rubbish listed in the poem was found on a beach in winter. Do you think the same sort of litter would be left during the summer months? Make a list of rubbish you might find on a summer beach.

- Take the children on a walk to your local river, stream, nearby pond or beach. Ask them to make a list of all the rubbish that they come across. Take photographs of polluted areas to display in the classroom.

- Use the lists of rubbish as a word bank to write a list poem, in the style of 'Jetsam'. Display the poems on large outlines of bottles, cans or tyres.

- Use information gathered on the walk to plan a pollution collage. Paint background paper with murky blues and greens, and add water-weed and stones, using paints or collage materials. Model bottles, cans and tyres from self-hardening clay, allow to dry and then paint and varnish. Glue the clay pieces to the collage. Perhaps a swimmer could be added, unaware of the pollution beneath!

- Plan a pollution survey for local residents. Think of questions you would like answers to, such as 'Are enough rubbish bins provided in the area?' 'Are there signs warning people of the fines they will receive for dumping rubbish?' 'How can pollution problems in the area be solved?'

- Design signs for a clean-up campaign, either for the school pond or for a nearby polluted area of water.

- Write a letter to the local council complaining about the state of a local river, stream or other polluted area. Ask the children to set out their feelings in a reasoned and persuasive manner. Address an envelope correctly and design an anti-pollution stamp for the letter.

- Design a water pollution board game. Consider how the counters will be moved around the board, what will happen when you land on different squares and how the game is to be won.

- Design a beach pollution plaque to highlight the litter problem. Roll self-hardening clay into a rectangular slab, add coils of clay for the waves and press in small shells and pebbles to make the beach. Add bottle tops and bits of rubbish. Leave the plaque to dry, then paint and varnish.

- Read the story *One World* by Michael Foreman (Red Fox, 1992) in which the children realise the importance of looking after their world. In the story, the children make their own tiny world in a bucket. Give each child a paper bucket shape to create their own tiny sea world by adding collage seaweed, small pebbles, shells and a few fish and crabs.

- Looking into the rock pool, the children in the story (see above) are reminded about the beauty of the world and how easily it can be spoiled. How can we keep the beaches clean so that they remain places of natural beauty? In what ways do people spoil our beaches?

Creatures of the Deep

It is so dark at the bottom of the ocean that some fish make their own light.

- Find out about the angler fish and other luminous deep-sea creatures.

- Using wax crayons, cover a sheet of paper with several layers of luminous colours. Press hard to make the layers thick. Finish with a layer of solid black. Use a pointed tool to draw the outlines of unusual deep-sea fish into the black wax. The luminous colours will show through. Bend a wire hanger into a fish shape and attach the fish to the hanger. Add coloured beads for eyes and suspend the fish in an under-the-sea display.

- Use diluted PVA glue to fix overlapping coloured tissue-paper pieces on to black plastic bags. Cut out fish shapes and peel from the black backing. Tape to wire hangers.

Deep-sea fish tend to eat one another as there are no plants in this sunless world. They have enormous mouths and long back-curved teeth for grabbing and eating anything that swims by.

- Model deep-sea fish from self-hardening clay. Add cocktail sticks for the sharp teeth and jewels, beads or pearls to represent the glowing lights that many of them create. Paint and varnish the models.

Hundreds of fish glow in the dark of the deep sea, making their own light through a process known as bioluminescence. Some glow all over while others have a pattern of light spots.

- Create a glowing fish by making pinholes in aluminium foil that has been mounted across a cardboard shoebox frame. Display against a window so that the light shines through the pinholes, making a glowing fish outline.
- Deep-sea fish have quite ugly distorted faces and some interesting names, such as viper fish, lantern fish and slickhead. Using pastels, sketch imaginary deep-sea fish on black sugar paper and create new and interesting names for them.
- Away from the shore, the ocean plunges to over 3 kilometres in most places. The seabed is covered in huge cracks called trenches. Research some of the creatures that lurk in these deep-sea trenches. Use information books, encyclopedias and the internet.
- The oar-fish is the longest fish in the ocean, at roughly 12 metres. Find out about some other ocean record breakers, such as the smallest fish, the biggest type of seaweed and the largest crab.
- The largest crab is Japan's giant spider crab which is roughly 4 metres across from claw to claw. Make a giant spider crab by covering a bowl and eight cardboard legs with papier mâché. Coat the bowl with petroleum jelly before applying the papier mâché so that the bowl is easily released. When hardened, paint an orange-pink colour and join the legs to the body.
- The fastest fish is the sailfish which can swim at over 100 kilometres per hour. Research and sketch the sailfish, with its long pointed nose, on black card and add details using pastels. Create a record breakers display.
- Write an acrostics poem about one of the unusual deep-sea creatures. Begin each line with the letters of its name. For example:

    Slickheads

    Swimming in the depths
    Luminous dots glow
    Incredible sharp teeth ...

Dance, Drama and Music

Dance

- Use Courbet's painting *The Wave* to capture the mood of the sea through dance (see page 28). Work on the gentle ebb and flow movements of the tides and contrast them with the strong, turbulent, crashing and rolling movements of the waves.

Drama

- Read Judith Nicholls' poem 'Put on your Thinking Hat!' (see page 25). Use the poem as a drama warm-up activity to focus on questioning. Begin with one child putting on their hat and asking the others a question which must be answered by a mime.

- Read the story of 'Amana and Her Children' (see page 21). Talk about the emotions that are evoked in the story – love, jealousy, envy, anger and fear. Work in pairs and make up a short sketch to convey one of the emotions.

- Act out one of the emotions addressed by the story, for example jealousy. (The Sun was jealous of all the new stars and planets that Amana had created, and Tamula was jealous of his brother being chosen to create the first people to inhabit the Earth.)

Music

- Use the painting *The Wave* as inspiration to compose your own music. Consider the mood of the painting. Is it calm and relaxing or wild and turbulent? What instruments would you use to capture the waves? Will you play them loudly or softly, fast or slow? Can you invent your own simple method of notation to record your musical composition? Perhaps use symbols associated with the sea.

Earth

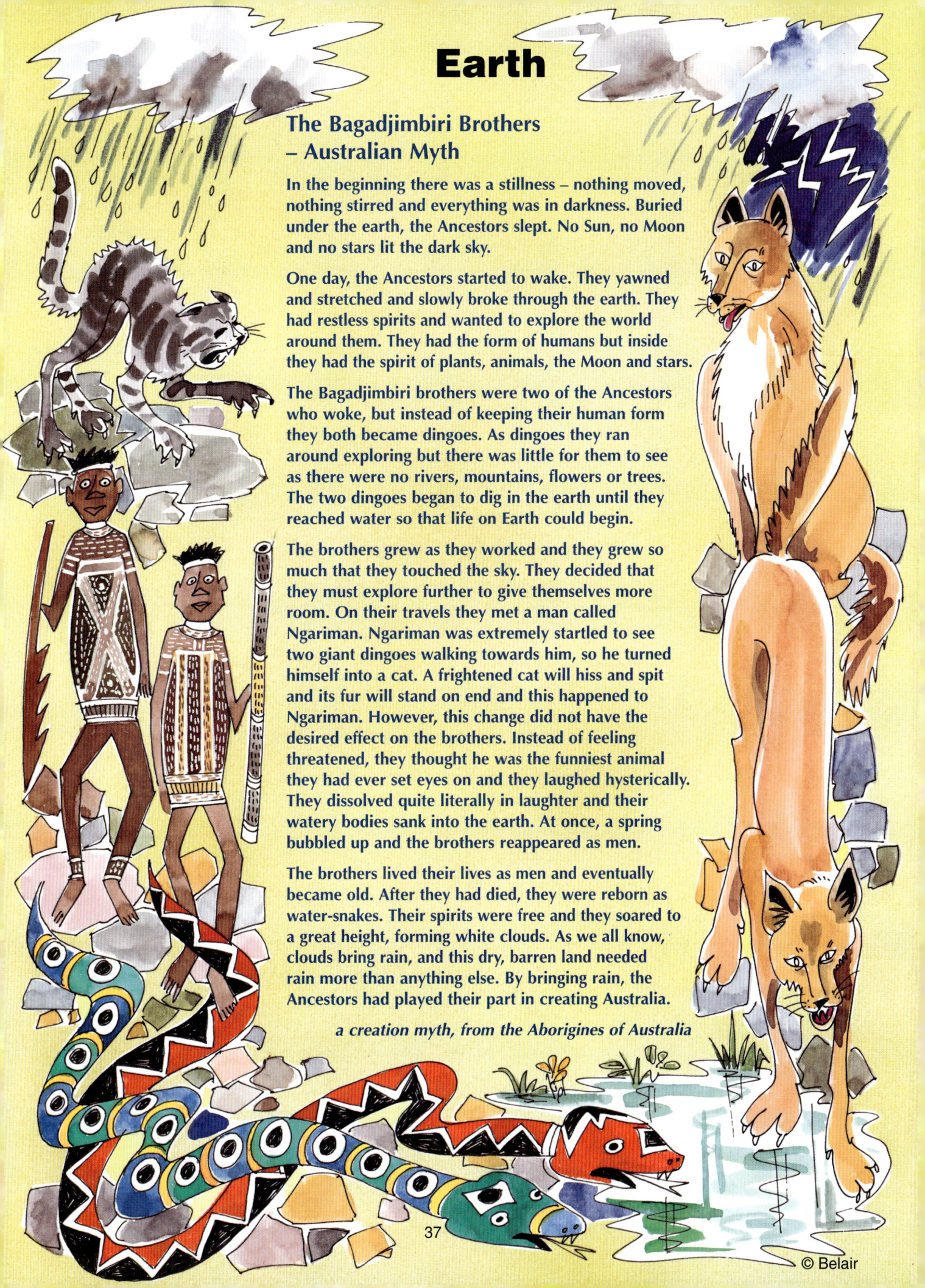

The Bagadjimbiri Brothers – Australian Myth

In the beginning there was a stillness – nothing moved, nothing stirred and everything was in darkness. Buried under the earth, the Ancestors slept. No Sun, no Moon and no stars lit the dark sky.

One day, the Ancestors started to wake. They yawned and stretched and slowly broke through the earth. They had restless spirits and wanted to explore the world around them. They had the form of humans but inside they had the spirit of plants, animals, the Moon and stars.

The Bagadjimbiri brothers were two of the Ancestors who woke, but instead of keeping their human form they both became dingoes. As dingoes they ran around exploring but there was little for them to see as there were no rivers, mountains, flowers or trees. The two dingoes began to dig in the earth until they reached water so that life on Earth could begin.

The brothers grew as they worked and they grew so much that they touched the sky. They decided that they must explore further to give themselves more room. On their travels they met a man called Ngariman. Ngariman was extremely startled to see two giant dingoes walking towards him, so he turned himself into a cat. A frightened cat will hiss and spit and its fur will stand on end and this happened to Ngariman. However, this change did not have the desired effect on the brothers. Instead of feeling threatened, they thought he was the funniest animal they had ever set eyes on and they laughed hysterically. They dissolved quite literally in laughter and their watery bodies sank into the earth. At once, a spring bubbled up and the brothers reappeared as men.

The brothers lived their lives as men and eventually became old. After they had died, they were reborn as water-snakes. Their spirits were free and they soared to a great height, forming white clouds. As we all know, clouds bring rain, and this dry, barren land needed rain more than anything else. By bringing rain, the Ancestors had played their part in creating Australia.

a creation myth, from the Aborigines of Australia

Aboriginal Australian tradition says that their people have animal, plant and human ancestors who created the world and everything in it. This process of creation is known as Dreamtime. Through singing, dancing and chanting at festivals such as Corroboree young Aborigines learn about Dreamtime. The people taking part paint their bodies with elaborate patterns.

- In this story the Bagadjimbiri brothers changed from their human form into dingoes and Ngariman turned himself into a cat. Ask the children to imagine that they could change into an animal. Which animal would they choose to be? Write about the advantages of being this particular animal and give reasons for their choice.

- Aborigines traditionally believe that although Dreamtime happened thousands of years ago, it is still with us today. Use information sources to discover more about Dreamtime and the Aborigines' beliefs.

- In the story the dingoes dissolved quite literally in laughter. Find other expressions that can be taken literally, for example, let the cat out of the bag, jump the gun, caught red handed, head in the clouds. Explain the meaning of each expression and draw a picture to demonstrate how each can be taken literally.

- Try to catch the spirit of Dreamtime in a wax-and-ink painting. Use a pencil to draw a scene from the Dreamtime story 'The Bagadjimbiri Brothers' on a square of white cotton material. Draw over the lines with a white candle, pressing hard. Paint over the wax using a suitable selection of coloured inks and allow to dry. The wax will resist the ink and the white candle lines will stand out. Iron the material between sheets of white sugar paper.

- Use dough to make Aboriginal figures to add a three-dimensional aspect to the painting (see page 69 for dough recipe). Bake the figures in the oven. Allow to cool and then paint and varnish. Remember to decorate the figures with traditional Aboriginal body patterns.

- The Bagadjimbiri brothers were two of the Ancestors who awoke from their Dreamtime, while buried under stones and earth. Decorate stones and pebbles in the style of Aboriginal art, by covering them with white Plasticine and pressing in different kinds of pasta and pulses.

Aboriginal tradition says that all Aborigines belong to a clan – a large family that their Ancestor created. Each clan is named after an animal, and so an Aborigine could belong to the emu, the wombat or the dingo clan, for example. An Aborigine would never hunt the animal that gave the family clan its name. At a corroboree festival the clans gather together to sing and dance. The men dress up and paint their faces and bodies and the children learn the sacred songs of their Ancestors.

Corroboree

The clap, clap, clap of the clapstick beat
By the old, red rocks with their scar
To the stamp, stamp, stamp of the old men's feet
And the wink, wink, wink of the stars.
With the drone, drone, drone of the didgeridoo
And the sound of its ancient tune
In the dance of the snake and the kangaroo
By the light of the walkabout moon.
The chants will rise and drift and fall
While the night with a magic fills
Where the old men dance to the Dreamtime's call
In the heart of the secret hills.

Max Fatchen

- Read the poem 'Corroboree' and find the phrases in the poem that reveal the time of day when the festival takes place. How many clues can you find?

- Look for evidence in the text which suggests the location of the festival. Use this information to draw a picture of the scene.

- The 'red rocks with their scar' refers to Ayers Rock, called Uluru by the Aborigines. Find out why this place is of special significance to Aborigines.

- Identify from the poem how the music is made. Find out what type of instruments the clapsticks and didgeridoo are.

- Make clapsticks from wooden blocks and decorate with Aboriginal-style dot patterns using cotton-wool buds and paint. Varnish when dry.

- Use the poem to inspire paintings of Aborigines dancing under a starry sky with snakes, kangaroos and other Australian animals. Paint the picture on sandpaper for a textured background.

- Make up rhythmic chants to say at a corroboree festival. Use clapsticks, other home-made instruments and stamp your feet as accompaniment. Make up a clan name and use your particular animal in a chant.

Gods of the Earth

Many cultures think of Earth as a mother goddess and the source of all life. All our food is either grown in the soil or comes from animals which depend on the earth for their food. Around the world people give thanks and celebrate when the earth yields a good harvest. In some countries, people pray to the earth god or goddess and shrines are built in their honour. Hindus call the mother goddess Shakti. Shakti is sometimes fierce and sometimes kind. In her fierce form she is known as Kali and her gentle side is called Parvati.

- Ask the children to consider the fierce and kind sides of their own character. When and why does their nature change? Draw two different profiles on a head shape and in each side describe the fierce and kind sides to their character. Can they give each side a different name?

The Ibo people are from Nigeria, Africa. Traditionally, their most important crop is the yam and to make sure that they have a good harvest they pray to the Earth goddess, Ale. The Ibo place little red and blue painted clay figures called Ale dolls around each planted yam to make it grow well. When they are harvested a shrine, called the Mbari house, is built for Ale. The square house has a thatched roof and a veranda around it. The pillars inside are painted with patterns and the shrine is filled with brightly painted clay figures of Ale, her brother the storm god and her sister the water goddess. Colourful cloths are also hung inside the shrine.

- The most important crop for the Ibo people is the yam. Find out about yams and how they grow. Try to find a traditional African recipe using yams.

- Make Ale dolls using clay. Paint them red and blue, and glue on small beads for eyes.

- Make a shrine to the goddess Ale to give thanks for a successful harvest. Use a cardboard box for the shrine and veranda, and cardboard tubes for pillars. Decorate the walls and pillars with colourful geometric patterns and add clay figures of Ale, her brother the storm god and her sister the water goddess. Cover the roof with real straw or art straws painted yellow.

The Greek Earth goddess was Demeter, the sister of Zeus. She was the goddess of grain and fertility. The fields, meadows, flowers and herbs were all under her protection.

The Greeks tell a story about Demeter which explains why our seasons change.

Demeter had a daughter called Persephone who was kidnapped and taken to the underworld by Hades. Demeter wandered the Earth searching for Persephone and when she was unable to find her she cursed the Earth so that all the plants began to wither, the fruits shrivelled and the leaves turned brown and fell from the trees. Finally a bargain was struck so that Persephone spent half of the year with Hades and then returned to the Earth for the other half. On her return, buds burst into flower and trees were green once again. This, the Greeks tell us, was the start of spring and the beginning of the seasons.

- Tell the story of Demeter and Persephone. Identify which seasons fall into the time that Persephone spent with Hades. Describe how the Earth changed when Persephone left Hades to return home.

- Make up stories to explain how the seasons began and why they change.

- Create a collage of Mother Earth, perhaps as a sleeping woman covered with a large patchwork blanket of fields. Make the Earth blanket by painting different fields. Scratch or print crop designs onto the fields and add pressed flowers and leaves. Cut the fields into hexagons and assemble them to make the patchwork blanket. Add a pillow with a border of pressed flowers and leaves, and paint the face of Mother Earth.

The Maori people of New Zealand tell the story of Papa, their Earth goddess. Papa and Rangi, the sky god, were so much in love they would not let go of each other. Because the Earth and sky were always joined, no light could enter the world. Their children tried to separate them and eventually one of their children, Tane, managed to push his body between them. The parted parents cried and their tears became great rivers and seas. To stop the world flooding, the children turned Papa over so that Rangi could not see her sad face and now the only tears are the dewdrops you see on the grass each morning.

- Tell the story of Papa and Rangi. Write your own descriptions explaining how the Earth goddess and the sky god might be separated.

- An Egyptian story tells of the sky goddess Nut, who could not be separated from the Earth god Geb. Read accounts of the story and discuss how it differs from the story of Papa and Rangi.

Mythical Earth Creatures

There are many strange and wonderful creatures described in myths and legends. Some of the most well known include the centaur, the faun, the unicorn, the sphinx and the chimaera. The centaur and the faun are creatures in Greek mythology. The centaur has a man's head and body, and the legs of a horse. The faun has a man's body, a man's head with two little horns, the legs of a goat with hooves, and a tail. Fauns were thought to haunt lonely places and those who felt their presence were often gripped by fear and fled in a panic.

- Find out why people believed centaurs really existed. Research and write about Chiron, the wisest and oldest of the centaurs.

- A faun called Mr Tumnus features in *The Lion, the Witch and the Wardrobe* by C S Lewis (Prentice Hall & IBD, 1986). He told tales of nymphs and dryads and wild red dwarfs. Make up your own story including all these creatures.

- Narwhals have a long spiral horn just like the horns unicorns are thought to have. Find out what a narwhal looks like and how it uses its horn. Draw sketches of these animals.

- The unicorn is believed to have magical powers over water and is said to clean polluted water by dipping its horn into it. Imagine a unicorn was recently spotted in your local park. Write a story telling how this unicorn was able to help deal with today's pollution.

- A unicorn and a lion are on the British royal crest. Design a coat-of-arms for your own or another country. Include mythical beasts in the design.

- Make a print of a mythical earth creature such as a unicorn. Draw a unicorn on a polystyrene circle or tile using a pointed instrument. Prick along the lines of the design, then paint over the polystyrene with white poster paint and print onto black paper.

- Work in groups to make the shape of a large unicorn from modelling wire. Use spiralled cardboard for the horn. Cover with papier mâché and paint white. Attach a bunch of white plastic strips for the tail and add details for the eyes and mouth. (See pulp recipe and photograph on page 70.)

The Egyptian sphinx has a human male head and the body of a lion. The Greek sphinx has a woman's head, eagle wings and the tail of a serpent as well. This sphinx would lie in wait to accost all passing travellers. It would ask a riddle and those travellers who solved it were allowed to pass but those who failed were killed and eaten. The sphinx asked: 'What animal is it that in the morning goes on four legs, at noon on two and in the evening on three?' The answer was 'man' – who crawls as a baby, walks as a man and who uses a stick in old age.

- Can you solve the riddle of the sphinx to save your life?

- Make up your own riddles that the sphinx might ask passing travellers.

- Design a sphinx with an animal head and a human body.

The chimaera is a Greek mythological fire-breathing monster, with a lion's body and three heads: the head of a lion and a goat, and another head – of a serpent – as its tail.

- Sketch some three-headed creatures. Base them on known animals or invent your own. The most successful ideas could be modelled in wire and papier-mâché (see page 70 for papier-mâché pulp recipe).

- Imagine coming face-to-face with a chimaera. Write an account for a local newspaper. Include an eye-catching headline to make people want to read the article, for example: 'Three-headed Monster Spotted In Local Woods', 'Don't Go Down To The Woods Today Unless You Want A Terrifying Surprise', 'Two Heads Are Better Than One – But I Saw A Creature With Three!'

- Work in groups to design a pack of mythical beast playing cards. Include eight mythical earth creatures (two families), eight mythical sea creatures, eight mythical fire creatures and eight mythical creatures of the air. Use the cards to play 'Mythical Beasts Families', 'Snap' or 'Pairs'.

Painting Landscapes

Vincent van Gogh (1853–1890) was fascinated by the cypress trees in the south of France and he painted them many times, often emphasising their writhing, flame-like shapes. He worked for several hours every day, setting up his easel outside and working in the burning sunshine or freezing winds.

Van Gogh painted thick layers of colour, applying paint so liberally that individual brushmarks were ineffective. He resorted to squeezing paint straight from the tube onto the canvas and modelling it a little with his brush. The dashes and swirls seen in his paintings became his trademark, although it was only in the last two years of his life that van Gogh painted in waves and swirls that were applied so thickly they stood above the canvas.

- Use van Gogh's *Wheatfield with Cypresses*, 1889, for reference and practise his techniques of painting with dashes and swirls. Use poster paints mixed with PVA glue and a little flour to produce a thick and shiny oil painting effect.

- *Wheatfield with Cypresses* shows a beautiful swirling sky – indeed, it is difficult to find straight lines anywhere in the painting. Paint a simple landscape of land and sky in van Gogh's style using paint mixed with paste. Apply the paint with your fingers to achieve the flowing swirls.

- Van Gogh's paintings have a wonderful sense of movement and colour. Paint a landscape, perhaps one that surrounds your home or school, using van Gogh's style to capture the urban or rural environment.

- Read *Camille and the Sunflowers* by Laurence Anholt (Frances Lincoln, 1995) which shows how difficult life was for van Gogh with little money and few friends. Write about his struggle to become a successful artist. Did he achieve success in his lifetime?

- Van Gogh's painting *The Sower with Setting Sun*, 1888, is effective partly because he limited his colours to violet, yellows, oranges and blues. Work with a limited palette and paint on silver foil which has been scrunched-up and then flattened out over a board. (Don't screw up the foil too tightly or it will be difficult to flatten out again.)

- Van Gogh painted landscapes at night as well as those bathed in bright sunshine – one of the most famous being *The Starry Night*. Paint your own evening landscape in the style of van Gogh's.

- Look at the landscape work of artist Georges Seurat and compare his style to van Gogh's. Van Gogh painted his landscapes with bold dashes and swirls. Seurat did not blend his colours on the palette but applied dots directly onto the canvas leaving the final blending to the eye of the onlooker – a technique known as pointillism. Try painting a familiar landscape in a pointillist style.

Harvest Festivals

People around the world celebrate when the harvest is gathered in. In Israel there are three different harvest celebrations each year. At the festival of Sukkoth in the autumn, Jewish people make huts from leaves branches, flowers and fruit to remind them of how their people lived after fleeing Egypt and how God looked after them and provided food. They often eat their meals in the hut for the eight or nine days of the festival and on the final day there is singing and dancing.

- Put up a world map in the classroom and talk about how the harvest is celebrated in different countries around the world. Research how the harvest is celebrated in a given country and prepare a short presentation for the rest of the class.

- To remember the time spent in the desert by their ancestors thousands of years ago, a special Sukkoth service is held in the synagogue. Everyone holds branches from three different trees in their right hand. Research and write about the significance of these plants.

- Design a stained-glass window for a synagogue showing branches from the palm, willow and myrtle, as well as flowers and fruits gathered at harvest time.

- Find out about the other Jewish harvest celebrations, Pesach or Passover and Savuot.

In the United States of America, Thanksgiving Day is celebrated each year to remember how the first Pilgrim settlers cultivated their crops and made new lives for themselves. American families celebrate Thanksgiving with a meal that always includes corn, as that was the first crop harvested by the settlers.

- Plan a celebration meal for Thanksgiving, including corn, turkey and pumpkin pie. Make and decorate menus with a border of fruit and vegetables.

- The first white settlers in North America celebrated their first harvest by inviting Native Americans to join them in a thanksgiving feast. Native Americans had taught them how to grow the native crops and so helped them to survive their first winter. Find out which crops were native to North America and draw pictures of two very different harvest suppers – one set in 1621 and one in modern day America.

It is a Mexican custom to place fertility figures in the crop fields as a prayer for a good harvest.

- Look at Mexican crops such as sweetcorn, sweet potatoes, beans, coffee, mangoes or bananas. Design an appropriate fertility figure for each crop. Fold a sheet of coloured paper in half, then draw half the figure against the fold line. Cut out and unfold to reveal the complete figure. Use contrasting coloured paper for mounting the figures and display in a patchwork pattern for a strong visual effect.

The Dogon people from Mali, West Africa, celebrate a good harvest by performing special dances in large animal masks decorated with wool, feathers, leaves and shells. The masks are often as much as a metre high.

- Make a harvest mask by gluing material onto a cardboard background. Paint a scary face onto the material, then decorate with feathers, shells, small pieces of bark, pressed leaves or wool. Paint turtles, lizards and crocodiles on hessian, mount on card and then staple to the top of the mask, one above the other.

In Britain, harvest festivals are mainly celebrated in Christian churches. In the past, fruits were taken in procession to the temple in baskets decorated with flowers and leaves. Today, baskets of fruit and vegetables are collected in schools and churches to thank God for his goodness.

- Make papier-mâché fruit and vegetables for a harvest display. Make the frame with thin cardboard and newspaper and hold it in position with masking tape. Use diluted PVA glue to stick torn strips of newspaper over the shape. Leave to dry and then paint and varnish it. Display the fruit and vegetables in decorated boxes and baskets.

- Plan a harvest supper to celebrate harvest festival. Find recipes and write menus that include seasonal fruit and vegetables. Add decorative borders appropriate to the harvest theme.

- Write a short poem or prayer of thanks for the harvest.

The Polluted Earth

Who Made a Mess?

Who made a mess of the planet
And what's that bad smell in the breeze?
Who punched a hole in the ozone
And who took an axe to my trees?

Who sprayed the garden with poison
While trying to scare off a fly?
Who streaked the water with oil slicks
And who let my fish choke and die?

Who tossed that junk in the river
And who stained the fresh air with fumes?
Who tore the field with a digger
And who blocked my favourite views?

Who's going to tidy up later
And who's going to find what you've lost?
Who's going to say that they're sorry
And who's going to carry the cost?

Steve Turner

- Read the poem 'Who Made a Mess?' by Steve Turner. Discuss the issues raised in the poem and identify the ways in which we are destroying our planet.

- The poet uses lots of questions in the poem. Work in groups to discuss and provide possible answers to the questions.

- Write a series of six questions that you would like to ask about pollution. Begin each question with 'who', 'which', 'when', 'why', 'where' or 'what'. Examples: 'What can be done about pollution?' 'Why have we allowed the Earth to become such a mess?' 'Which countries deal with pollution in the best way?' Use information sources to find answers to your questions.

- Write an additional verse for the poem 'Who Made a Mess?' Follow the same format, asking questions and rhyming the second and fourth line.

- Make up an imaginative spring-cleaning list to clean up the planet. For example:

  1. Hoover the fields
  2. Dust the buildings
  3. Polish the stars
  4. Sieve the sea.

  Choose one item from your list to illustrate and paint.

Recipe for Disaster

- Write a 'Recipe for Disaster' showing some of the destructive things we are doing to our planet.
- Write a 'Recipe for Success' to show ways in which we could look after our world.

Recipe for Disaster

1. Take one planet.
2. Add a few power stations.
3. Add more and more new roads and several airports.
4. Stir in some polluted water.
5. Add tropical hardwoods from the rain forests, mixed with vehicle exhausts.
6. Cut down some more trees and sprinkle on top.
7. Cook with the heat of the sun through a hole in the ozone layer.

This is a recipe for disaster.

Valerie Evans

- Design a 'Save the Earth' booklet. Make a zigzag book with circular pages to represent the world. On the cover, draw the continents of the world and fill the booklet with ideas on how to look after the Earth for future generations.
- Talk about how an area of wasteland could be changed into a beautiful wildlife garden to play in. Design and plan a wildlife garden for an area of wasteland in or around your school.
- Try recycling some rubbish with the class. Set up collection points for paper, cans and glass. Design posters to encourage more people to recycle.

Animals in Danger

- There are many species of animal which are in danger of disappearing from the Earth. Find out which animals are in danger and which are already extinct. Make notes about a particular endangered animal.

- Write the notes in a hexagonal lift-the-flap book. Draw a picture of the animal on the front. Put the hexagons together in a tessellation to represent the shell of a turtle. Stick the hexagons down so that each flap can be lifted to reveal the written information about the animal underneath.

- Make hexagonal tiles from clay. Draw an endangered animal on a rolled-out piece of clay, and then cut it out using a clay tool. Join the animal to the tile with slip so there are no visible joins. When dry, paint and varnish.

- Tessellate the children's tiles to represent the shell of a turtle. Grout or glue them onto a large piece of plywood. Add the turtle's head and limbs. Paint the bare areas of the board with PVA glue and sprinkle with sieved sand.

- *Turtle Bay* by Saviour Pirotta (Frances Lincoln, 1998) tells the story of a man's efforts to clean beaches and watch over the loggerhead turtles that come ashore to lay their eggs. Read the story to find out why loggerheads and six other species of sea turtle are endangered species.

- Ask the children to imagine they are an animal in danger of extinction and that they have to write a persuasive letter to plea for their survival. Why do they consider that they are worth saving? Why will the world be a poorer place if they die out altogether?

- Draw an endangered animal on a piece of card and cut it out. Cover in papier-mâché (see page 70) and allow to dry and harden. Finally, paint the animal with poster paints.

- Write appropriate similes to display alongside the papier-mâché animals, for example:
  - As rare as a rhino
  - As endangered as an elephant
  - As threatened as a tiger
  - As precious as a panda
  - As protected as a polar bear.

- In China there are only 800 giant pandas left. Find out how the Chinese government is addressing the problem. What action is being taken to increase the numbers of other endangered animals?

- Start a 'Save the Seal' campaign in school. Send off for information packs and write to the World Wide Fund for Nature.

- Design and make a badge for an endangered animal. Look up information on the internet.

- Paint endangered animals on pebbles using poster paint, then varnish.

Dance, Drama and Music

Dance

- The Dogon people from Mali, West Africa, celebrate a good harvest by performing dances wearing large animal masks. The masks are often decorated with crocodiles, lizards and turtles. Make up a dance of celebration using music from *Spirit of African Sanctus*, track 21 'Bwala Dance' (original recordings by David Fanshawe).

- The Corroboree is an Aboriginal celebration in which clans named after different Australian animals get together to play music, sing and dance. Work in groups, named emus, wombats, dingoes, snakes and kangaroos. Each group must make up a celebration dance in which it is clear which animal group they are representing by the way they move. Use Aboriginal music or let each group make up their own music, for example using clapsticks, shakers and stamping their feet.

Drama

- Make animal masks of threatened species. Use the masks in a drama activity in which the children take on the roles of different animals who meet to discuss their future and their chances of survival on Earth. Ask the animals to express their worries and concerns about the issues that affect them most. For example, Cheetah: 'I can't run as fast because the air is so polluted'; Panda: 'Farmers are clearing the forest to plant their crops and so there's not enough bamboo for me to eat'; Elephant: 'Illegal hunting and poaching still goes on and I'm always in danger. People still want jewellery and ornaments made from my beautiful ivory tusks.' Can the other animals make suggestions as to how to deal with the different problems?

Music

- Make musical instruments using pots, tubes and boxes filled with beans and pulses. Attach handles made from cut lengths of cardboard tube. Cover with at least three layers of kitchen paper strips and PVA glue. When dry, paint bright patterns on the instruments, then varnish.

- Make up some rhythmic chants to say at a corroboree festival and use clapsticks and home-made instruments as an accompaniment. Each group of children can make up a clan name and use their particular animal in a chant.

- Compose a rhythm for the poem 'Corroboree' by Max Fatchen (see page 39) and sing rather than recite the verse.

Air

Loawnu Mends the Sky – Chinese Myth

In the beginning, the world was new but not everything was perfect. There was a problem with the sky.

One day in China, when a group of children were out playing, blue lumps of different sizes began raining down on them. At first they couldn't think what was happening but when they looked up they realised that pieces were falling out of the sky. When the pieces fell, holes were left in the sky and it looked very strange. The children couldn't think how to solve such a problem but then one child suggested visiting Loawnu, the oldest and wisest woman in the village.

Loawnu thought that she would be able to help if the children returned to the fields where they were playing and collected all the pieces that had fallen from the sky. The children did as they were asked, but when they took the pieces to Loawnu she told them that there were more holes than pieces of sky. 'I'm sure that some pieces have fallen where they can't be reached,' said Loawnu. 'Perhaps some have fallen to the bottom of the ocean where nobody can reach them. I can put all these pieces that you've collected back into the sky but we will need to think of something to fill in the gaps.'

The children all sat and thought but nobody had an idea of how to solve their problem. One of the children began kicking at the coloured stones on the ground in front of her. 'That's it,' said Loawnu. 'We'll use these beautiful red, pink, purple, orange, yellow and green stones to fill in the holes. The sky will look more beautiful than it's ever looked before.'

The children's faces fell. 'What's the matter?' asked Loawnu. 'You asked me to solve your problem and I have.' 'We don't want a multi-coloured sky,' said the children together. 'The sky is blue – we want a blue sky that turns black each night.' Loawnu promised the children that when they woke up the next day the sky would be as blue as the bluest ocean. 'Now I have work to do to mend the sky and you must all go home to your families,' she said.

The next day all the children were delighted to see a beautiful clear blue sky with no holes at all. They weren't sure just how Loawnu had mended the sky and she wouldn't tell them. 'I think she used magic paint,' said one child. 'Or beautiful blue material,' added another. The children played happily in the fields that day under a bright blue sky.

When evening fell, the children, worn out from their play, fell fast asleep. Only one child tossed and turned, unable to sleep. Finally, she got up and walked to the window where she met an amazing sight. The sky wasn't plain black, it was glistening and sparkling with silver light – Loawnu had filled in each hole in the sky with a dazzling silver star. The little girl shouted so loudly that the whole village came running and as nobody had seen stars before they were all amazed. The villagers loved watching the stars glitter and twinkle and some stayed up all night, watching until the sky finally turned blue. Now everyone knew how Loawnu had mended the sky.

a creation myth, from China

- Read the story 'Loawnu Mends the Sky'. The children in the story thought Loawnu had used magic paint or beautiful blue material to mend the sky. Think of other ways in which the sky could have been mended. List the different possibilities.

- Make a tissue-paper collage to tell part of the story. Use diluted PVA glue to stick torn pieces of tissue paper to black plastic bags. Overlap the tissue paper to make new colours and make sure that no gaps are left. Cut out stars and cover with silver glitter or silver spray. When dry, peel the pictures from the plastic bags, add silver stars and display in a window for a wonderful translucent effect.

- Paint colourful designs on beach pebbles to be used to fill the gaps in the sky. Varnish and display alongside the children's pictures.

- Draw a picture of how the sky would look with beautiful coloured stones filling all the gaps.

- Loawnu promises the children that she will make the sky as 'blue as the bluest ocean'. Think of similes to describe the colours of the stones that Loawnu suggested using to fill the holes. For example, 'as yellow as the sun on ripe corn' or 'as pink as the pinkest ballet shoes'.

- Write a story similar to 'Loawnu Mends the Sky', but begin with the children playing in the fields one evening and the Moon falling out of the sky. How is the Moon returned to the sky? Who helps the children solve their problem?

- Talk about how strange it would be if pieces started falling out of the sky. Adopt the roles of the children in the story and interview them about their strange experience. Plan questions such as: 'What did you think was happening when lumps began raining down on you?' 'Were you very frightened?' 'What action did you and your friends take?'

- Write newspaper articles about this strange event and think of eye-catching headlines.

- Some pieces of sky may have fallen to the bottom of the ocean. Make a list of interesting and imaginative ways that these could be retrieved, for example an octopus using all eight legs could collect the pieces and bring them to the surface.

- What is a star? Use information sources to find out about stars. Display this information on cut-out star shapes. Hang them in front of the tissue-paper collage pictures (see page 54).

Gods of the Air

There are many mythical gods of the air who claim responsibility for the thunder, lightning and freak weather conditions experienced on Earth. Thor, the Norse god of thunder, creates storms by whirling his hammer in the air. He is often shown riding through the air on a chariot, pulled by two huge billy goats! Pots hanging from the sides of the chariot clash and clatter, making the sound of thunder.

Thor

Tonight, Thor, god of thunder
Is riding through the sky
Listen as his wagon
Rumbles by

When he flings his mighty hammer
Watch the sky turn black
See the lightning flashing
Hear the thunder crack

Eric Finney

- The poem 'Thor' by Eric Finney mentions the god's mighty hammer which was known as Miollnir. Thor had three great treasures, the other two being a belt, which when worn doubled his strength, and a pair of iron gloves to wear as he wielded the hammer. Add two more verses to the poem mentioning Thor's other treasures and continuing the rhyme pattern.

- Flame-haired Thor, with his mighty hammer, belt and gloves, riding a chariot pulled by two goats through the sky must have been quite a sight! Paint a picture of Thor using the poem for inspiration.

- The god Thor gave his name to 'Thorsday' which eventually became Thursday. Find out who the other days of the week were named after.

- Think of new names for the days of the week, linked to the sky in some way. For example, Moonday, Cloud-day, Rainday, Thunderday, Fogday, Summerday and Stormday.

The Hindu sky god is called Indra. One day, Indra was being chased by the demon king Ravana. A peacock suggested that Indra should crouch down low and hide behind his tail feathers. Ravana rushed past without seeing Indra and Indra was so pleased that he transformed the peacock's dull brown plumage into brilliant blue, green and purple with a golden eye on each feather. As Indra the sky god was the bringer of rain, people now regard the peacock's cry as a sign that a storm is on the way.

- In India, wandering storytellers used to carry long picture scrolls to help them tell their stories. Tell the story of Indra and the peacock in a series of pictures painted on the back of a roll of wallpaper. Make decorative Indian borders with strips of wallpaper. Use the scroll to tell the story to other children.

Varuna, the Hindu sky god, is believed to know absolutely everything because he has a thousand eyes and is all-seeing. Varuna flies through the sky but travels in the sea on the back of Makara, a beast that is part dolphin, part shark and part crocodile.

- Varuna is all-seeing because he has a thousand eyes. Draw an eye to put on Varuna's head. Write about what this particular eye sees, for example 'I watch the sea creatures with this eye' or 'I keep an eye on the weather!'
- Draw a picture of Makara. Don't forget that it is part dolphin, part shark and part crocodile.

There are several Japanese gods that control the wind and weather. Haya Ji, the god of typhoons, carries the wind around in a leather sack and releases it to punish humans. Raiden, a Japanese thunder god, is portrayed as a red demon with horns on his head and claws on his feet. He makes the sound of thunder by banging loudly on drums.

- Write a story about Haya Ji releasing typhoons from his sack by mistake and causing havoc on Earth. Write about the damage caused and how Haya Ji eventually captured the typhoons and returned them to the sack with the help of Raiden, the thunder god.
- Find a picture of Haya Ji and use an overhead projector to project the image onto a large sheet of paper. Draw around it and complete the fearsome image using oil pastels.
- Find and record as much information as you can about typhoons. Display the work on typhoon shapes and swirls escaping from Haya Ji's sack.
- Hurricanes are given names, for example 'Hurricane Gertrude' or 'Hurricane Harry'. An alphabetical list of names is drawn up each year for that year's hurricanes. Make up 26 names for hurricanes – one for each letter of the alphabet.

Mythical Creatures of the Air

A griffin is a monster with the body of a lion, the head and wings of an eagle and the pointed ears of a dog. It is used to pull the chariots of the gods. It is eight times bigger than a lion and is said to patrol the skies keeping watch over gold mines and areas of buried treasure. With the strength of a hundred eagles, it can easily carry off a full-sized horse which it regards as an enemy. The bodies of griffins vary in colour, from white to golden yellow, with wings of brown or bright blue.

- Listen to the description of the griffin above. Its appearance, strength and mission are described. Draw a picture of the griffin from the description given.

- Imagine the griffin patrolling the skies and suddenly seeing several dark figures entering an Egyptian tomb full of golden treasures. What might happen next? Can you continue this story?

Pegasus, the beautiful winged horse of Greek mythology, was captured by the hero Bellerophon, with the help of Athene. The story tells how Pegasus was ridden up to the gods' home on Mount Olympus. Zeus looked down from the heavens and did not like what he saw and so sent a gadfly to sting Pegasus. This made the horse rear up, sending Bellerophon back down to Earth. Pegasus continued flying up to Mount Olympus and lived there forever after.

- Draw a cartoon strip that tells the story of Pegasus and Bellerophon. Include speech bubbles.

- Pegasus made Mount Olympus his home. Find out about some of the gods who lived there with him.

- Make a character screen. Sketch a mythical sky creature, based on Pegasus, Sleipnir (see page 59), or a griffin. Draw this large scale on paper and transfer to a sheet of MDF board. Paint with poster or acrylic paints and varnish.

- A griffin is part lion, part eagle and part dog. Create a new mythical creature perhaps called a niffirg or firfing by combining different elements from these three creatures!

Pegasus wasn't the only mythical horse riding the skies. Odin, the great Norse sky god, rode an unusual black horse with eight legs, called Sleipnir. He was accompanied by his two special ravens named Huginn (thought) and Munnin (memory). Odin was the god of war and knowledge. He only had one eye, having lost the other in return for absolute knowledge. Odin could change his shape and travel in the form of a bird or beast while his body appeared to lie sleeping.

- The ravens would fly through the air carrying messages to and from Odin. Write a message from Odin to the goddess Freya who drove a chariot drawn by cats, or to one of his sons, Balder, or the thunder god, Thor.

- Before going into battle, Norsemen would pray to Odin to keep them safe. If they died in battle they would be taken to Odin's palace. Write a prayer or letter to Odin, asking him to watch over you in battle.

Angels are often depicted in stained-glass window designs with feathery wings, flowing white clothes and gold or silver halos. However, there are also very different images, such as the angels in *The Nativity* by Julie Vivas (Voyager Books, 1994), who have torn clothes, tatty multi-coloured wings and hob-nailed boots.

- Look at how artists have represented angels over the years. Describe in detail and draw how you visualise angels.

- Find out about the different orders of angels. If you were a guardian angel, who would you want to watch over on Earth below?

- Make flying angels playing instruments or singing using the dough recipe (see page 69). Add wire hooks to the back of each model before baking for three to four hours. Paint with pearlised paints and add pipecleaners for halos.

Painting Skies

El Greco (1541–1614) usually painted religious paintings as he was an official artist for the Catholic Church in Toledo, Spain. *View of Toledo,* a landscape painting, was a change from his usual work. There is much to discuss in the painting – the stormy sky filled with black clouds, the castle and cathedral bathed in white light, along with the other buildings, and the ant-like textile workers washing cloth in the river. The exaggerated shapes and colours add to the drama of this atmospheric oil painting.

- Compare a number of different pictures and paintings of skies showing clear blue skies, cloudy skies, stormy skies and so on. Use El Greco's *View of Toledo* to promote discussion about different skies and the different atmospheres they create.

- Use El Greco's painting as inspiration to capture a stormy sky. Limit your palette to the colours seen in his painting, *View of Toledo*.

- Paint a small fresco (a wall painting, painted directly on wet plaster), inspired by El Greco's *View of Toledo*. Plug the corners of a shallow cardboard box with Plasticine. Put water into a bowl and slowly add plaster of Paris, stirring until it becomes a creamy consistency. Once it begins to thicken, pour it into the shallow cardboard box. Allow to harden to an interesting lumpy and textured appearance. While the plaster is still damp, paint a stormy scene using the bumps to emphasise the stormy sky.

- On a warm cloudy day, lie on the grass and watch the clouds moving across the sky. Look for different types and shapes of clouds and make sketches. Experiment with colour-mixing shades of blue sky.

- Draw clouds on grey paper with a white wax crayon or a white candle. Paint over them with a blue colour wash. This resist technique can be very effective when painting skies.

- Use watercolours to paint a blue sky. While the paint is still wet, dab with small pieces of cotton wool or a dry brush to remove the paint and leave cloud shapes.

- Create the effect of a 'heavy sky' by painting a wash using two shades of blue, with the darker shade above the lighter shade.

- Paint a rainy sky by painting clouds and then dabbing off paint along the bottom edges. Add straight, grey lines coming down from the bases of the clouds.

- Paint a polluted sky. Use a thick brush or small sponge to wet the paper all over. Starting at the top, paint strips of dark grey, purplish blue, greyish green and so on, letting the colours run into each other. When dry, add buildings and factories belching out swirls of smoke.

- Experiment with painting purple skies or a red and orange sunset sky, blurring the colours together. Blurring is easier to achieve if the sky is painted onto wet paper. To paint a sky with texture, try adding some washing powder or sawdust to the paint.

- Paint humorous skies to illustrate well-known phrases or sayings, for example 'a mackerel sky' or 'raining cats and dogs'.

⚠ **Note:** Do not study the sky when weather conditions are bright or sunny. Never look at the Sun.

Festivals of the Air

In Japan, on 5 May, all the schools are closed because it is Children's Day. The festival used to be called the Boys' Festival while the girls had a special day on 3 March called the Dolls' Festival, but now the two festivals have been combined. On 5 May kites shaped like carp fly from all the homes where there are children. Children are told to battle against difficulties and to be brave, just like the carp.

- Kites are often flown at different festivals. Ask the children to design their own kite. Ask questions such as 'What shape of kite flies best?' 'What are the best materials for making a kite?' After completing some designs test them out and see which kite performs best on a blustery day.

- Make carp kites from cotton material. Draw the fish shape on a folded piece of material, cut out and decorate with fabric pens or three-dimensional paint. When dry, put the decorated sides together and stitch around the edge of the fish. Turn the right way out and sew in a wire loop to keep the fish's mouth open. Hang from bamboo canes.

- How would you celebrate Children's Day? Plan a festival to be held in your town or village and write a timetable of the day's events.

- Japanese children are told to battle against difficulties and be brave like the carp. Ask the children to choose an animal that would show their strengths. Ask them to write down instructions explaining how to make their particular animal mascot to hang outside their home.

Each year at the Bristol balloon fiesta in England hot-air balloons take to the air, virtually filling the sky with colour. Often, over a hundred beautifully coloured balloons rise into the sky. The balloonists take part in 'Hare and Hound' chases where one particularly bright balloon is chased across the sky by many other balloons. There are other aerial displays, too, with helicopters and microlight planes.

- Make papier-mâché hot-air balloons by covering inflated rubber balloons with glue and paper strips. Allow to dry, and then decorate in original ways. Hang small baskets underneath, containing all the details about the balloon fiesta to advertise the event.

- Make a plaster of Paris plaque showing a balloon fiesta. Pour water into a bowl and gradually stir in the plaster of Paris until the consistency is creamy. Plug the corners of a cardboard box or use a wooden box. Slowly pour the plaster mix into the box and leave to harden. Paint a design of colourful hot-air balloons on it while the plaster is still damp.

- Imagine how it would feel to go up in a hot-air balloon. Write about your imaginary feelings on a cut-out balloon shape.

Ancient Aztec warriors, called voladors, used to 'fly' at one of their religious festivals. Wearing bird costumes, they would jump off the top of a high pole. The ropes they were tied to were attached to the pole so they whirled round and round through the air before landing. The ceremony represents the Sun moving in the sky and is still performed in Mexico today.

- Cut out and decorate card figures of the voladors in their bird costumes and attach each to a pole with a piece of string. Display the voladors whirling around the pole.

- Find out more about the voladors' 'flying' ceremony. Imagine how it would feel to be a volador who is about to perform at a festival for the first time. Write a description of your feelings, such as the possible mixture of excitement, nervousness, fear and pride.

Air Pollution

I Need A Gas Mask

When I walk around town,
it's really busy
and the smell of car fumes
makes me dizzy.

When I go in the cafe
for a drink and a cake,
the cigarette smoke
makes my head ache.

When I sit on the bank
where the river flows,
the smell is so bad
that I hold my nose.

When I stand near the factory
and the wind's from the south
it stings my eyes
and blows grit in my mouth.

With all these horrible
things in the air,
I need a gas mask to go anywhere.

Charles Thomson

It is getting more and more difficult to take a 'breath of fresh air' in today's world of car fumes, smoke from chimneys and waste from factories. Air is the most easily polluted of all the elements.

- Read 'I Need A Gas Mask' by Charles Thomson. List all the sites and sources of pollution he identifies in his poem.

- Suggest possible actions that could be taken to combat the effects of pollution, for example only drive your car on certain days of the week.

- Copying the format of the poem, write an additional verse starting 'When I ...'. Rhyme lines two and four in the same way.

- Draw pictures to represent the different polluted scenes in each verse of the poem.

- Divide a sheet of card and draw two scenes inspired by the above poem. The scene should be the same on each, but with one as a clean, pleasant environment and the other as a polluted environment. Divide and cut each picture into seven equal strips. Then glue the strips, one from each scene alternately, onto a sheet of card that has been concertina-folded into 14 matching-sized strips. When complete, the polluted scene can be seen from one angle, while from another angle a cleaner world will be visible. (See photograph on page 4.)

- Read *Tower to the Sun* by Colin Thompson (Red Fox, 1999). The story is about the air becoming so polluted that it is no longer possible to see the Sun and aircraft can no longer fly in the polluted skies. Discuss the transport shown and the way that people travel in the story.

- Look at the illustrations in the book to identify some of the famous buildings used to build the tower to the Sun. Use information sources to find out about these buildings, such as when and why they were built, who designed and built them, and what they are used for.

- Make a list of other possible ways the boy and his grandfather could have tried to reach the Sun.

- Make dough houses and famous buildings using the dough recipe on page 69. When joining details onto the buildings, put water on the part to be added. Bake the finished items on baking trays for three to four hours at 150°C and leave in the oven until cool. Paint and varnish the buildings. Attach coloured Cellophane to the windows.

- Make a background for the dough buildings by painting a murky sky on wet paper. Add the Sun at the top where the sky has cleared. Display the buildings in the form of a tower.

- The tower to the Sun was built at Ayers Rock, called Uluru by the Aborigines. In which country is Uluru and why is it considered such a special place? Do you think it was a good place to build the tower? Why?

- Write a newspaper article about the construction of the tower to the Sun and all the famous buildings being used. Report on how the tower is progressing and include a punchy, eye-catching headline.

- Imagine that you are in charge of assembling the tower to the Sun. Make a list of jobs to be done and equipment needed, for example arrange the collection and shipping of the buildings from their original sites, organise forty enormous cranes for lifting and so on.

Creatures of the Air

There are thousands of different birds but millions of different flying insects. Lots of these flying creatures have special talents. For example, dragonflies can lay eggs while flying and can even fly backwards. Humming birds can also fly backwards and hover to feed, beating their wings up to 100 times a second! Many birds eat while flying and some even sleep on the wing. Bats are the only mammals that can fly and many use radar guidance to sense the world around them because their eyesight is poor.

- Select a flying creature from the bird or insect group. Try to find the particular superstars in each group, for example super size, super speed, super flier and present the information in a zigzag book.

- Make a 'creatures of the air' mobile. Draw butterflies, birds and bats on thin folded card, colour and suspend from a hoop, varying the lengths of cotton for added interest.

- The ostrich has wings but cannot fly. Find out about flightless birds and explain why each particular bird is unable to fly.

- Cut out butterflies from folded white paper. Open out and press flat. Wet the butterflies with a small sponge and drop watercolour paint on to the shapes – the colours will run and merge to make interesting patterns. While the paint is still wet sprinkle salt on some of the butterflies to create an interesting textured effect.

- Cut out dragonflies in the same way and colour with marbling inks. Drop the inks on to a tray of water with a pipette. Swirl around to create an interesting pattern. Place the dragonflies on to the pattern, lift off and allow to dry.

- Model dragonflies from self-hardening clay. Push pipecleaners into the soft clay for the wings and legs. Paint the models with pearlised paint. Varnish when dry.

- Make a pond using torn tissue paper for the water and add fish cut from orange paper. Cover the pond with plastic bubble wrap for a watery effect.

- Make a large pond collage to display the dragonflies and butterflies. Add bulrushes made from sandpaper with marbled paper leaves. Place clay dragonflies and frogs around the pond on sand, rocks and stones.

- Study the way in which insects fly. Look at the different shapes of insects' wings and note how quickly or slowly they fly. Which insects have two pairs of wings and which have only one pair? Make notes and sketches about each insect studied.

- Make simple wax-and-ink batiks of insects. Draw an insect on paper with a wax crayon. Colour the insect and background with thick wax crayon layers, covering the whole sheet. Screw up the work into a ball, being careful not to tear the paper, then flatten the work out and paint over the whole picture with coloured drawing ink. Make sure that the ink goes into all the cracks. Finally, iron the picture between sheets of clean white sugar-paper – the results should be stunning.

Dance, Drama and Music

Dance

- Storms were once said to be caused by the thunder gods being angry. Build up a sequence of bold heavy movements to represent thunder and contrast them with fast, sharp, darting movements to create lightning. Combine the thunder and lightning movements and put them to the music 'Mars' from *The Planets* 1917 by Gustav Holst.

- Work on 'flight' movements, including taking off and landing. What body shapes can you make in the air when in flight?

- Listen to *The Flight of the Bumblebee* by Rimsky-Korsakov. Think about how you might move to the music to imitate the movements of a bee. Can you make up your own insect dance entitled 'Flight of the Dragonfly', 'Flight of the Butterfly' or 'Flight of the Ladybird'?

Drama

- Read the story 'Loawnu Mends the Sky' (see page 53). Act out the section of the story in which the children are playing in the fields and blue lumps of different sizes rain down on them. What should the children do? Whom should they tell? What can be done to mend the sky? Attempt to solve the problem with the children's own ideas.

- Conduct television interviews with the children. Ask questions such as 'Did you feel that the world was ending?' 'How did you feel when lumps of sky began to fall on you?' 'How can you explain this unusual occurrence?'

Music

- Listen to Beethoven's 'Storm' from Symphony No 6, Movement 4 Allegro while looking at the stormy painting *View of Toledo* by El Greco. Can you identify the strings as rain and the piccolo as the howling wind? What instruments are used as the full strength of the storm is unleashed?

- Experiment with instruments to find the most suitable for composing their own stormy music. Create a slow-brewing storm that gradually builds into an explosive and violent storm. Discuss how the music 'Storm' inspired their own composition. Perform their compositions to an audience.

- Sit in a large circle and, without using instruments, gradually build a storm by rubbing hands together to represent a gentle breeze, with the children following one after another. Continue rubbing hands and then begin quietly to say 'plop, plop', one by one, for the sound of raindrops. Begin patting knees as the rain becomes heavier. Finally, stamp feet to represent thunder and make swishing noises with the mouth for the strong winds of the storm. Continue the actions in reverse as the storm dies down.

Recipes and Methods

Dough Recipe

Materials

2 mugs of plain white flour
1 mug of finely ground salt
335ml of lukewarm water
Mixing bowl

Cup
Clay modelling tools
Rolling pin
Non-stick baking trays

Method

1. Pour the flour and salt into the mixing bowl and mix well.
2. Gradually add sufficient water and knead the mixture into a ball for at least ten minutes as this makes the dough pliable and easy to work with.
3. Model the dough on a lightly floured surface.
4. Place the dough models on a non-stick baking tray and bake in the oven at 150°C (300°F, Gas mark 2). Small items should be baked for 1½ to 2 hours, larger items for 3 to 4 hours.
5. Leave the dough models to cool in the oven.

Papier Mâché Pulp Recipe

Materials

Newspaper   Sieve   Saucepan
Mixing bowl   Cup   Wooden spoon
Hot water   Whisk   Flour and water paste or PVA Glue

Method

1. Cut or tear several layers of newspaper into small pieces and fill the mixing bowl.
2. Soak the paper in hot water for three hours and then knead into a pulp with your fingers.
3. Put the pulp into a sieve and squeeze out the water – the pulp can be stored in a plastic bag in a refrigerator until needed.
4. Mix a cup of flour with a cup of water and whisk.
5. Add two more cups of water and whisk to a smooth paste.
6. Heat the paste mixture in a saucepan and bring it to the boil stirring constantly. (This will need adult supervision.)
7. Allow the paste to cool before using with the paper pulp.
8. Add a tablespoon of the flour and water paste mix or PVA glue to the pulp and knead well until the mixture feels pliable and easy to model with.

Tie-dye Methods

Materials

Bucket
Cold water dyes
Packets of fixative
Salt
String
Rubber bands
Marbles, shells, coins, corks, stones

Method for clump tying

- Tie in a stone and criss-cross with thread. Bind along the loose fabric at intervals for a rippling circular effect (a).
- Tie stones, marbles, shells, coins or corks into the fabric for circles (b).

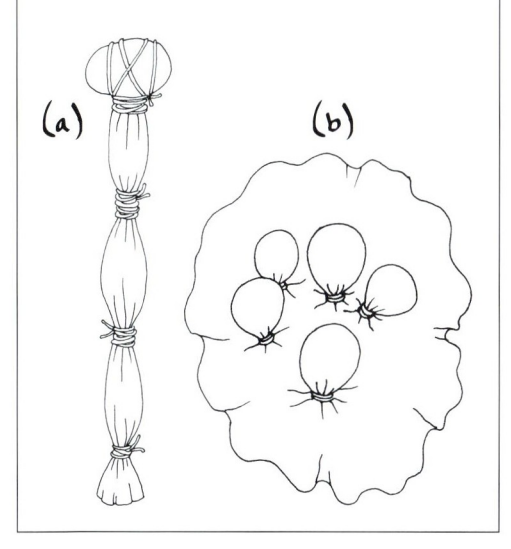

Method for twisting and coiling

- Twist the fabric tightly so that it coils back on itself. Bind at ends and at intervals along the skein.

Method for pleating

- Gather the fabric in regular folds and bind tightly at close regular intervals.

For details of further Belair publications,
please write to Libby Masters,
BELAIR PUBLICATIONS LIMITED,
Apex Business Centre,
Boscombe Road, Dunstable, LU5 4RL.

For sales and distribution in North America and South America,
INCENTIVE PUBLICATIONS,
3835 Cleghorn Avenue, Nashville, Tn 37215,
USA.

For sales and distribution in Australia,
EDUCATIONAL SUPPLIES PTY LTD,
8 Cross Street, Brookvale, NSW 2100,
Australia.

For sales and distribution (in other territories),
FOLENS PUBLISHERS,
Apex Business Centre,
Boscombe Road, Dunstable, LU5 4RL,
United Kingdom.
Email: folens@folens.com